To Wes,

To a Great Dresser,

love!
Angie

BEST IMPRESSIONS IN HOSPITALITY

BEST IMPRESSIONS IN HOSPITALITY

Your Professional Image for Excellence

ANGIE MICHAEL

IMPACT PUBLICATIONS

MANASSAS PARK, VIRGINIA

Library of Congress Cataloging-in-Publication data

Michael, Angie, 1948–
        Best impressions in hospitality: your professional image for
excellence / Angie Michael.
            p. cm.
        Includes bibliographical references.
        ISBN 1-57023-018-8
        1. Hotels—Employees. 2. Restaurants—Employees. 3. Clothing and
dress. 4. Beauty, Personal. 5. Grooming for men. 6. Self
—presentation. I. Title.
TX911.2.M53 1995
647.94'068'3—dc20   95-11718
                                                            CIP

Manufactured in the United States of America
1 2 3 4 5 6 7 8 9 10 98 97 96 95

For information on distribution or quantity discount rates, Tel. 703/361-7300, Fax 703/335-9486, or write to: Sales Department, IMPACT PUBLICATIONS, 9104-N Manassas Drive, Manassas Park, VA 22111-5211. Distributed to the trade by National Book Network, 4720 Boston Way, Suite A, Lanham, MD 20706, Tel. 301/459-8696.

This book is dedicated to George, my husband, whose continuous love and support has enriched my personal life with happiness and growth. His vision, his faith in my potential and his encouragement have been the foundation for my professional success in this country. *Mr. Wonderful, this book is for you!*

TABLE OF CONTENTS

CONTENTS

VIII

THANK YOU VERY MUCH!

*W*henever I start a seminar, a presentation or any business meeting, the above words are the first I always say. And this is how I want to begin this book. Thank you very much to:

Pam Leigh, my dear friend whose remarkable editing skills helped me to craft every idea in perfect English, making this an easy-to-read book. Pam, your support and contribution to the entire project was invaluable; the endless hours you kept polishing the writing, conducting research, and many more things that made this book a reality. I could have never done this book without your help. It is great fun working with you. Thank you very much!

Ron and Caryl Krannich, my publishers. You give new meaning to the author-publisher relationship and pleasant team work.

My dearest clients and friends at Colonial Williamsburg Hotel Properties, Inc.: James C. Miles, John T. Hallowell, Robert J. Jeramiah and their teams. Thanks for all the years that you have used my services as an educator for your hotels' employees. Special thanks to Brian O'Day, Bob Cox and Paul Freiling for your cooperation with the cover of the book, created at Colonial Williamsburg.

All my hotel and resorts clients around the country, so many to name. Thanks for giving me the opportunity to serve you and to learn the world of hospitality.

The Virginia Hospitality and Travel Industry Association, the Hotel Association of Washington D.C. and the American Hotel and Motel Association. You each have welcomed me as an allied member of your associations, giving me the opportunity to learn and to present to your members my message over the years. Thanks for your support!

The Association of Image Consultants International for the honor of my serving on the international board. I appreciate your confidence and support. I hope that this book will contribute to our commitment to the professionalism of the image consulting industry.

Craig Snow and Chris Miller from Cornell University. You made the first steps of the project workable and fun.

I am so fortunate to have many colleagues who are also true friends—always willing to listen, encourage, share ideas and provide vital feedback. I am deeply grateful for your wisdom, generosity and support. Jeanne Churchwell, my partner and friend—you have supported me through my image work for many years. Norah Hoff, Ann Frees, Hope Sage, Marina de Eusse, Oscar Navarro, my dear friends, thanks for the years of learning and laughter. My life is enriched—as is this book—because of you. My dear friends from the Image Growth Group—you held the vision of this book with me along the way. Mary Elizabeth Kaiser, you went the extra mile to help with whatever I needed throughout this project.

Mary Spillane my dear friend and colleague from England, you have been an inspiration to me. Thanks for keeping me updated on the European corporate culture and trends on professional image and hospitality.

Thanks also to Monica Nuemann, Steven Barnett, Mary Jane Barnes and Cheryl Birch for reviewing specific chapters.

All the illustrations and photographs in the book are the result of the enthusiastic participation of several companies dedicated to excellence. Having your materials available made this book a reality: Hartmarx Corporation, Barrie Pace Ltd., Angelica Uniforms, JoS.A.Bank, Colonial Williamsburg Hotel Properties, Inc., Britches of Georgetown and Uniforms To You. Special thanks to Michael Frank and your team at Uniforms To You. Your commitment to this book has a special place in my heart.

And, finally, my deepest gratitude to Keri Nikol, my Office Manager. Thanks for "keeping the ship afloat" while I was immersed in this book. Your help, time and assistance made it all possible.

NOTES FROM THE AUTHOR

*I*f you work in any area related to the hospitality business, this book is for you. Hospitality is more than a profession, it is a lifestyle. It is a challenging and exciting career that involves not only skills, but your whole person. In a global society things are changing so fast that we need to keep up not only with the latest technology, but also with the new ways to relate to our multi-cultural customers and coworkers. First impressions in hospitality are critical. Encounters are brief and lasting. The way you look, what you say, how you say it and what you do have a significant impact on the people you work with and the people you serve.

With your over-busy schedule, you probably don't have the time or energy to study the many books on each subject that pertain to first impressions and professional image. This book will make the task easier. Whether you are a manager who leads employees, or a team member who serves internal or external customers, you will find a complete set of guidelines for all aspects of your professional image: your appearance, grooming, clothing, uniforms, body language, verbal communication, customer relations and business etiquette.

The chapters on professional dress offer internationally accepted guidelines for business dress for men and women and how to select clothing and accessories to be appropriately and well dressed

for every occasion. The chapter on uniforms includes guidelines on how to wear your uniform with class. The chapter on grooming applies to everyone. The chapter on hospitality includes the ins and outs of body language, words, voice and actions that make or break the service excellence cycle. There is a chapter on business etiquette for those who conduct business and entertain clients in offices, meeting rooms, dining rooms and at conventions. It includes guidelines for all situations from how to make appropriate introductions, how to treat male and female colleagues and clients and how to conduct business and entertain clients at the dinner table. These guidelines will give you the confidence that comes from knowing how to handle any business situation. If selecting uniforms is one of your responsibilities, the last chapter describes a system that will facilitate this sometimes cumbersome process.

MY ROLE IN HOSPITALITY

My love for hotels started early. My 15th birthday celebration was at a hotel in my home town in my native Colombia. After the party I asked my mother if I could move to the hotel permanently! I loved everything: the people were very nice, everyone was happy and helpful, the food was great and, besides, I didn't have to make my bed! (That is still a treat today.) My teenage dream came true. For the past 15 years, since I moved to the United States and became involved in the hospitality industry, I have practically lived in hotels and restaurants. During these years, I have traveled extensively within the United States, Latin America and Europe for pleasure and for work.

My work with hospitality began in the early '80s. My previous experience as a management trainer and an image consultant were the stepping stones to my work in hospitality. I began to conduct our trademark Image Impact Seminars on Professional Dress and Business Etiquette to hotels and resorts from coast to coast. In the mid-1980s I developed the only program available that combines "appearance and customer relations" for uniformed employees. Most of my knowledge about the industry has come from the hundreds of participants I have met in my presentations and seminars conducted for hospitality associations, hotels and resorts of all sizes around the country. I have had the privilege of not only delivering these seminars, but also training other image consultants internationally to deliver Image Impact Seminars. Their experience has also contributed to the body of knowledge that I am pleased to share with you in this book.

Whenever I finish a session, my audiences always want more information. When we are presenting appearance, they have questions on etiquette; if we are discussing customer satisfaction, they want guidelines on grooming, and vice versa; and managers want advice on how to select new uniforms. Almost everyone is interested in getting up-to-date information on how to polish their professional presence and how to communicate better with others. This book is the response to my clients' requests.

I invite you to read this book with an open mind. You may focus initially on the chapters that suit your actual position. Hospitality offers great mobility so you may come back to the book when your responsibilities change or expand. I hope that you will have fun while gaining the knowledge to polish your professional image and to conduct yourself in any business situation feeling confident and self-assured. *Best Impressions in Hospitality* will show you how to maintain and communicate an image of excellence to navigate by in the 1990s with style and confidence!

BEST IMPRESSIONS IN HOSPITALITY

FIRST IMPRESSIONS

Make the right impression first,
by making the first impression right!

Like it or not, most people judge us by what they see. In the first few seconds of meeting, they have assessed us and made a judgment—positive or negative—that is not easily changed. Before they even hear what we have to say, they have formed an impression. In fact, by the time we open our mouths to speak, our words will account for only a portion of a person's perception of us. The rest is based on our tone of voice and the way we look and move.

When we first meet someone, we look for clues such as clothing choices, grooming and demeanor to tell us about their trustworthiness, credibility, effectiveness, cleanliness, attention to detail and more. These inferences and responses are a part of being human; we need to simplify and organize the incredible amount of stimuli coming at us day and night. These clues are also a shortcut to evaluating a business establishment. By observing the appearance and body language of the personnel, a customer judges—again, positively or negatively—whether or not he or she wants to do business there.

It's obvious, then, that personal appearance, grooming, body language and the first words we say are tools that we can use to influence the visual impact that we make during our first moments with a new person. When we understand how much we influence others by our dress and appearance, we become much more careful in selecting what we wear to face the world each day.

Our "high-tech, low touch" world

In this decade of globalization, we live in a society that has been called "high-tech, low touch." In other words, most communications are done through electronics and machines. Face-to-face encounters are usually brief and, therefore, their effectiveness depends on how well and accurately we get our message across. We simply cannot afford to wait for a *second* positive first impression.

And certainly nowhere is it more important to immediately present a professional business image than in the hospitality industry. When we work in this industry, we are in the "people business" and our encounters are brief. Thus, in the eyes of the customer your personal appearance and the service you provide represents the image the client has of the company. How you dress and present yourself can affect your effectiveness, your profitability and, therefore, your career and the company's success.

The fancy, four-color brochure a hotel, motel, restaurant or resort uses for advertising may entice a prospective guest to visit or stay overnight, but it's the staff's appearance and behavior that will encourage repeat business. The public buys "perceived value." And when, for example, hotel employees look trustworthy, efficient and impeccable, most guests assume that the property is equally trustworthy, efficient and impeccable, too. For the customer, *you are the company.* Therefore in this decade, with the emphasis on quality and employees' empowerment, companies realize that attracting and keeping customers is a process that begins and ends with their employees.

In addition to the potential impact that clothing, grooming and manners have on the viewer, we must also factor in the impact that these choices have on the wearer as well. Pride in your appearance contributes to your sense of self-worth. Studies on this subject link clothing consciousness to higher self-esteem and job satisfaction. According to research by Dr. Judith Walker, Farleigh Dickinson University, it is in your best interest to put effort into accentuating your "positive visual image." When we know we look appropriate and we know how to conduct ourselves in any business situation, we feel comfortable and empowered and can concentrate on the business at hand to achieve our goals.

*"In the '80s we dressed for success,
in the '90s we dress for excellence."*

Dress, especially business dress, is more than our public skin. It is language. We live in a symbolic environment where virtually all the symbols we learn are acquired from others—our family, the country we are raised in, our peers, the company we work for and the work we do. Clothing defines and describes us to the world. That is the reason we wear uniforms: so we can be identified as members of the particular team dedicated to serving our client's needs. The ten percent of our body not normally covered by clothes is comprised largely of our face and hair. This is the critical ten percent since this is where people first look. Therefore, our grooming and clothing define the messages that we send out daily about ourselves.

Clothes do not necessarily make the man or woman. But clothes and behavior definitely influence a person's perception of us. Since both our clothing choices and our body language speak eloquently about us, we can use these "tools" at our disposal to positively enhance our visual impact. After all, our ability to successfully convey our message depends on it. William Thourbly, author of *You Are What You Wear,* maintains that "your appearance is truly the one factor you can control. If you package yourself to manage the impressions you make on others, then their positive reinforcement will, in time, make you the person you want to be."

Beyond appearance: what you say—what you do

The elements of image excellence do not stop at clothing and grooming issues. A positive first impression goes beyond how we look (appearance) and what we do (body language) to the way we communicate and serve others. Today we face many challenges: our customers vote everyday with their money when they choose our property. Satisfying our value-driven customer is not enough to succeed in today's competitive market. We need to delight the customers and exceed their expectations. The relationship between men and women has certainly changed dramatically in the past few years. Some of the graciousness that was appropriate in social settings, has been modified in the work place. These changes, plus the new ways of communicating with each other through high-tech devices, have brought a new set of rules of business behavior and etiquette.

In addition, in the hospitality industry, globalization is already here. We are multi-cultural—from the employees to the guests, from the clients to the suppliers. Ignorance of a client's particular culture is the surest way to unravel a carefully planned business relationship. The 1990s require a new international awareness, and in hospitality the responsibility is even greater. It is more than avoiding mistakes. It is knowing how to make the guest, the client, the employee and the coworker feel at home—to respect their values and cater to their customs to win their trust, loyalty and support. The global market gives us a great opportunity; after all, people from all over the world may be working with us and visiting us. It behooves all of us, no matter what our present work station, to be sensitive to their cultural differences.

Therefore, regardless of your position in the organization, whether you serve the guest directly or serve those who serve the guest, you are in the business of customer satisfaction. And the success of this process begins with the way you present and conduct yourself. Making the first impressions the *best and lasting impressions* will assure the excellence that you and your company promise and provide.

PROFESSIONAL DRESS FOR MEN AND WOMEN

*I*f you do not wear a uniform, your challenge as a hospitality professional is to communicate to the world, through your clothing and personal grooming, who you are. You probably will not brag about your credentials and achievements, but your clothing (along with your voice, words and behavior) will speak for you. As clothing normally covers 90 percent of our body, we need to be aware of exactly what our dress is communicating.

Whether you are in sales, management or on the "front line" serving guests and clients, your appearance, behavior and effectiveness on the job really do affect the organization's bottom line and, hence, your own bottom line. Even if your position is "behind the scenes" with no direct contact with the public, your appearance counts just as much as if you were at the front desk. In hospitality we are in the "people business," and our professional appearance is an essential element for excellence. Regardless of our position in the organization, our appearance must reflect quality, service and friendliness. A professional appearance gives us a sense of pride which we owe to ourselves, the customers and to our coworkers.

Achieving a professional image of excellence includes the art of selecting clothes that complement our physical characteristics and are right for our particular job and the company for which we work. And, of course, an important part of presenting ourselves with style and class is impeccable grooming.

The art of selecting the right clothes for business is a task that may be a challenge for many. Two years ago, we got a call from a company to meet with the CEO of a large corporation. When I walked into his office, I was prepared to meet one of the most powerful executives in the field of telecommunications. Imagine my amazement when the man who oversaw a multi-million dollar company with a staff of 7,000 employees warmly greeted me wearing khaki pants and a jacket from a suit, a striped sport shirt and a rumpled wool tie! Nothing went together! We know when clothing combines because all the pieces look like they are going to the same place. In his case, the pants were going to a picnic, the shirt and jacket to the office and the tie should have stayed home! When I sat down, he explained how difficult it was for him to manage his wardrobe: "I can handle my job easily, regardless of the challenge; my clothing skills stop at my closet."

So, as you can see, clothing uncertainty can plague anyone—from those just starting out in a company to the person who owns or manages it. Regardless of our position, we all have the challenge of selecting the right clothes for the right occasion. I am constantly approached in both business and social settings alike for advice on business clothing and appearance; sometimes people just want feedback on whether what they're doing is appropriate.

Selecting and wearing clothes for work is one of the few areas in business where we don't get much training or guidance. Most employee manuals in hospitality mandate that non-uniformed employees wear clothes that are "professional," but little to no description is given of what "professional" means. Many of us may get feedback that our appearance needs "polishing" and that we need to dress "more professionally." But even the supervisor who has the embarrassing mission of delivering this feedback does not instruct us in what clothing options will improve our image. This chapter will provide you with the guidelines—in clothing, accessories and grooming—to achieve your professional appearance for excellence.

DRESSING FOR A GLOBAL MARKET

In hospitality we dress for our guests, and our guests come from all parts of the world representing diverse cultures. Coupled with this globalization, we also have corporations downsizing their operations. As the pyramid-type configuration of the corporation hierarchy flattens due to this downsizing, the traditional power symbols tend to disappear. Therefore, the use of clothing to reinforce those messages and images of power has been changing to communicate messages of approachability and credibility. For example, in the 1980s the "power look" was the image of choice in most organizations, which made the accepted professional look quite predictable. We wore our "dress for success" suits and there was not much room for individuality. But as the world shrinks and borders "disappear," the cultural dress symbols become more international. In the 1990s we dress for excellence and quality. This creates more options and more creative alternatives to business attire, especially in hospitality. However, there are still guidelines that must be followed to ensure that the messages that we convey with our clothing are still professional. These internationally accepted guidelines for business will work for you whether you are working in the U.S. or abroad, and regardless of the clientele you serve.

In hospitality your dress symbols will be conservative and business-like, but with flair. Your attire needs to assure clients, guests, colleagues and suppliers that you are competent, but it must not create distance so that they are unwilling to share their concerns. Your goal, then, is to communicate both trust and credibility.

When my British colleague Mary Spillane was consulting with one of the largest hotel operators in the world, she found that "the management teams in London looked too severe and boring. They had to be reminded that they were in the hospitality business and based in a large metropolis, entertaining business people from around the world. More color was required for the women's suits and make-up and for the men's ties. In contrast, the staff from Amsterdam were all expensively dressed but too casual considering that their clients, again, were mainly business people." Both cities' staffs received very similar advice.

The guidelines presented in this chapter will assist you in being a well-dressed professional in hospitality. Being well-dressed means that you wear clothes and accessories that:

- complement your coloring and body type
- combine in color, fabric and pattern
- fit you properly
- are appropriate for the occasion
- reflect your personality and your position
- are current

COLOR AT YOUR SERVICE

One of the most critical elements in the selection of clothing is color. Using color properly will contribute in a big way to you looking your best. When there is balance and harmony between your own coloring—skin, hair and eyes—and your clothing, you look healthier, more alert and people notice you in a positive way. The right colors will help you project credibility, authority and accessibility. We have learned to associate some colors with power and formality and others with more informal and casual occasions; knowing which ones to choose helps us send appropriate messages.

There is more freedom today in the use of color in business than there was in the past, especially for women. But, regardless of this seemingly endless choice of colors for business attire, the standard responses to color that have been extensively researched still apply. Let's take a look at some of these time-honored responses and their accepted modifications.

Dark colors make one look more authoritative. For example, dark to medium gray and navy blue have always been preferred hues for those in a position of authority. But dark colors can also be intimidating, and they can overpower a person if his or her skin and hair coloring is light or medium. And black, while perfect for men's evening wear, is too dressy for the daytime. An exception to this rule, though, is that many women can benefit from black's strong color presence, especially if it complements her dark brown or black hair. It is too overpowering, though, for a light-haired woman. It is advisable, then, to learn just how dark a color you can wear so that you project authority, but are not overpowering yourself with the color. (In the next section of this chapter you will find guidelines on selecting the best colors for you.) Medium colors such as blue-gray or medium charcoal project less authority. They are better used for less formal occasions. They make you look more approachable, friendly and calm. When you need to establish rapport with a client you are meeting for the first time, wear a medium-tone outfit and save your more powerful dark and high-contrast look for closing a deal or negotiating money.

With an increased interest in the environment, earth tones—such as subtle brown patterns and tan in men's business suits—are more acceptable. However, brown and tan do not project the same credibility as gray or navy; therefore, it is best to wear them only in the summer or on those days when you do not have an important meeting.

Despite the popularity of pastel colors for women's clothing, professional women want to wear them with care. Pastel colors tend to be associated with social or intimate situations. They are more acceptable in warmer climates. However, when you wear them you need to be more assertive to project the same level of credibility as other colors provide. A touch of one of these shades—such as a handkerchief in a suit pocket or a blouse underneath a suit— would add pizzazz to your outfit without detracting from your professionalism.

Within these guidelines, there are more color options for business today. Men's navy and gray suits get a new, exciting look with colored threads and weaves in multiple shades that, at a distance, look like a solid but up close show understated flair. The infusion of green into traditional backgrounds of gray, navy and taupe adds a new vibrancy to suit fabrics. Also olive and other shades of deep gray greens offer another option for the hospitality professional. Keep in mind, though, that when choosing shades other than navy and gray, the fabric as well as the workmanship of the suit must be of exceptional quality; otherwise, you run the risk of looking ordinary and lacking in credibility.

Women at work are expressing their credibility with outfits that offer more variety than ever before: reds, from corals to burgundies to maroons; blues, from royal blue to turquoise to teal (the navy of the '90s); greens from emerald and jade to olive; and rich gold—all offer women new options in the business world.

Now let's look at which of these clothing color options are best for you. Most of us intuitively know that there are certain colors that we look and feel great in and some colors that make us look tired or even sick. When I show our seminar participants how I would look in a mustard colored suit (not a good color for me) they usually declare that I look sick and that perhaps we should call an ambulance!

Knowing the colors that complement you best not only helps you look healthier and more credible, it also helps simplify your shopping and dressing. The only sure way this kind of analysis can be done is by investing in a color analysis session with a Certified Image Consultant. One source for a color consultant is through your local yellow pages. Or call the Image Resource Group (phone number listed in appendix of this book) which maintains a roster of certified image consultants in most states.

In a private consultation, an image consultant trained as a color expert will assess your unique coloring and determine which colors will best enhance it. The consultant will explain the characteristics of your personal coloring and how to judge colors that will work for your business and casual wardrobes. To assist in this process, you receive a set of colored fabric samples in a wallet that you can use as a guide when you shop and select clothes for any occasion.

Although an individual color analysis is the most thorough and accurate way to gauge your coloring, there are some general guidelines that can help you select the best colors for you and avoid those that are not complementary.

YOUR COLORING
AND COLOR CHOICES

Your personal coloring is determined by your skin tone, hair and the color of your eyes. You can wear all types of colors but there are three qualities of the chosen color that must be in harmony with your coloring: the *intensity*—whether it is dark, light or medium toned; the *undertone*—true red, blue red or yellow red; and the *clarity*—bright and clear or subtle and muted.

We agree that a navy suit, a white shirt and a tie with a red pattern is considered a smart business outfit for a man. The questions are: How dark would you wear that navy suit? Would you choose a white shirt or an off white? What shade of red tie—red like a tomato or more like a burgundy?

For a woman, a navy suit and a colored blouse is also an appropriate business outfit. But do you select a dark navy or a grayed navy? Or would you prefer a gray-green or golden brown suit? Do you combine your suit with a pure white blouse, or would you look better in a cream or bright turquoise blouse?

Start by looking at yourself in a mirror and determine which of the following color categories suits you the best. It is often difficult for a person to "see" themselves—especially skin tone—but, to simplify, base your decision on your overall look, the color of your hair and the color of your eyes.

DEEP

OVERALL LOOK: Can be described as vivid with high contrast between the hair and skin.

HAIR: Dark—black to deep brown, chestnut, auburn and "salt 'n' pepper" as your hair gets grayer

EYES: Deep—brown, brown-black, rich green or olive but not blue

EXAMPLES: Sylvester Stallone, Whitney Houston, Bill Cosby, Cher, Diahann Carroll, Al Pacino.

Your coloring is considered Deep if you have a high contrast between the color of your eyes, hair and skin. Because of this contrast you can wear a comparable contrast in your clothing. For example, mix two dark colors together or a dark color with a light or bright color. Avoid an entire outfit with light or pastel colors in a monochromatic look. Use them for shirts and blouses only.

You should be aware that the people with Deep coloring with cool undertones look better in blue reds and burgundies and those with warm undertones should choose rust and warm reds. If you are Deep, a qualified image consultant will determine if you have warm or cool undertones.

Suggested Colors

MEN: Choose medium to dark navy and gray suits—charcoal is the best. White shirts, light blue, light gray, stripes with a white background. Dark or strong color ties in teal, true red, true blue, purple, terra-cotta, deep green, burgundy and turquoise.

Avoid: Light gray suits, golden brown, camel and taupe jackets. Be careful with earth tone suits—you may look sallow in browns. Avoid beige and yellow shirts.

WOMEN: Choose navy, black, charcoal gray, teal, royal blue, purple, true red, tomato red, terra-cotta and deep green suits and dresses. For blouses and accents select colors such as turquoise, coral and periwinkle. Black and white and black and red are good combinations.

Avoid: Light colors alone, bright oranges, light golden colors, most browns.

LIGHT

OVERALL LOOK: Fair coloring with medium to light contrast.

HAIR: Most often blond, light brown, ash or golden. If you are a woman you often highlight your hair to keep the blond look of earlier years.

EYES: Blue, blue-gray, blue-green, aqua, not deep hazel or brown.

EXAMPLES: Paul Hogan, Princess Diana, Linda Evans, Robert Redford

Your coloring is Light with light to medium contrast. When combining colors, select *medium tone colors and medium contrast.* Avoid colors that are too dark. Mix medium colors with light shades or other medium shades. Avoid colors that are too bright.

Suggested Colors

MEN: Choose navy or gray-navy suits—medium charcoal or charcoal blue-gray are best. You can wear camel or stone-colored jackets. Choose soft white and any pastel color shirt—blue is especially becoming—as well as soft stripes on a white background. Select ties in true blue, watermelon red, turquoise, yellow, lavender and a clear teal.

Avoid: Too dark shades of navy and gray, black and browns for suits; also ties in too dark or bright colors.

WOMEN: Choose medium navy, camel, blue-gray, charcoal blue-gray, cocoa, teal, blue-green, periwinkle, light royal blue, grayed-green for suits and dresses. Wear light tone blouses such as apricot, beige, off white, light blue or rose pink

Avoid: Bright colors that are too electric. Black is too strong but, if you decide to wear black, be sure to combine it with a light shade; black and red or black and a bright color will be overpowering on you.

WARM

OVERALL LOOK: Projects a total golden look with medium intensity.

HAIR: Medium range—blond or brown with golden, red or strawberry highlights.

EYES: Warm—green, hazel, brown, topaz, teal blue

EXAMPLES: Renee Poussant, Shirley Mclaine, Ted Koppel, The Duchess of York (Fergie), Cindy Crawford, Christy Turlington, Janet Jackson, Woody Allen.

Your coloring is Warm, meaning "gold undertones;" your skin, eyes and hair have a golden cast that must be complemented by colors of *medium intensity with golden tones.* Choose medium, not dark tones for suits; blended colors with some contrast are good. Enjoy the earth tones; they are your best colors. Avoid fuchsia, burgundy, pink, blue red and any rosy tone.

Suggested Colors

MEN: Medium charcoal, charcoal brown, medium navy, grayed-green, olive, gray with teal, rust and camel patterns. Shirts in ivory, off white, beige, peach and light yellow. Stripes in off white background. Ties in rust, teal, mahogany, tomato red, gray with gold and yellow.

Avoid: Dark navy or blue-gray suits, mauve or burgundy ties and pink shirts.

WOMEN: Golden bronze, camel, teal, grayed green, rust, mahogany, beige, marine navy, khaki, olive, tomato red suits and dresses. Ivory, peach, periwinkle, grayed-green and almost any shade of yellow or gold for blouses.

Avoid: Pink, burgundy, bright blues, blue-reds and pure white. If you love black, mix it with ivory, camel, beige or a golden tone.

COOL

OVERALL LOOK: Medium intensity with blue tones.
HAIR: Ash brown, blond or gray, silver or salt n' pepper.
EYES: Blue, gray-blue, rose brown
EXAMPLES: Bill Clinton, Paul Newman, Barbara Bush, Maya Angelou, Whoopie Goldberg, Eddie Murphy, Larry King.

Your coloring is Cool with medium contrast and your skin ranges from a pinkish beige to rose brown. You need medium contrast in your colors, and always look for *clothing with cool undertones* (tones of blue, burgundy and rose). Avoid any yellow or golden tones, brown (unless it is rose brown), camel or colors that are too strong such as black.

Suggested Colors

MEN: Any navy that is not too dark, blue gray, medium charcoal gray, gray with blue stripes or patterns. Shirts in white, soft white, any blue, pink, light gray or lavender. Striped shirts in navy or burgundy on a white background. Ties in blue-red, burgundy, plum, turquoise, gray-blue, mauve, medium purple

Avoid: Camel, black, olive and brown suits. Beige or yellow shirts or ties or any shade with golden tones.

WOMEN: Navy, gray, blue-gray, teal, charcoal blue-gray, plum, burgundy, blue red, blue-green suits and dresses. White, soft white, rose, lavender, periwinkle or any tone of blue or rose for blouses and accents.

Avoid: Browns (exception: rose brown), camel, ivory, yellow and golden tones. Black is too strong; if you wear it, mix it with soft white, light blue or rose.

BRIGHT

OVERALL LOOK: Projects a clear look with contrast between hair and skin tone.

HAIR: Medium to dark brown, black or rich gray

EYES: Bright and clear; jewel-like quality such as steel blue, blue-green, turquoise, black or brown that looks moist and clear

EXAMPLES: Michael Douglas, Maria Shriver, Connie Chung, Oprah Winfrey, Cristopher Reeve, Elizabeth Taylor, Naomi Campbell.

Your coloring is Bright and clear with a high contrast between your hair, skin and eyes. You need to continue this contrast in your clothing with *rich, bright colors and combinations.* Avoid muted or dusty tones and light colors used monochromatically. Wear true, primary colors. Mix dark with light or bright colors or wear two brights together. Avoid mixing two dark colors such as black and dark red; you always need a touch of bright or clear tone color in your outfit.

Suggested Colors

MEN: Navy from medium to midnight blue; medium to deep charcoal gray; blue-gray patterns; crisp pinstripes are excellent. White shirts are best; icy color shirts in blue, gray, pink, aqua. Ties in clear bold colors such as true red, turquoise, true blue, violet and purple.

Avoid: Brown and camel jackets; beige, cream or muted shirts and ties.

WOMEN: Navy, black, gray, charcoal blue gray, red, emerald green, turquoise, purple, teal, blue-green for suits and dresses. For blouses and accents, choose clear colors such as coral, white, lemon yellow, violet and deep periwinkle.

Avoid: Light colors—mix them with dark shades; camel and golden browns (use these colors only if they complement your hair); two dark colors such as black and deep purple may be too strong for you.

SUBTLE

OVERALL LOOK: Medium intensity coloring; a neutral look with medium depth.

HAIR: Medium range; medium to ash brown and ash blond; if gray, it is "mousy" not silvery.

EYES: Grayed green, hazel, brown-green, rose brown

EXAMPLES: Eric Clapton, Lloyd Bentsen, Queen Elizabeth.

Your coloring is Subtle, which means you have little contrast between the color of your eyes, hair and skin tone. You do not fit easily into any of the other categories; your coloring is blended and you need *blended colors of medium depth*. Wear medium contrast and avoid bright colors. Your color combinations will look boring on others but on you, subtle, muted combinations look elegant and sophisticated.

Suggested Colors

MEN: Medium charcoal gray, medium navy, pewter, charcoal blue-gray, gray with rust and teal patterns, rose-brown and olive suits. Shirts in soft white, light blue, beige, warm pink, light aqua; striped shirts where the background is not too white. Ties with tomato red, teal, mahogany, rust, grayed green, and any subtle shade.

Avoid: Too dark suits combined with white shirts and ties in clear colors; this kind of high contrast is overpowering.

WOMEN: Rose-brown, navy, blue-gray, teal, mahogany, deep blue-green, tomato red, deep periwinkle, olive, charcoal blue-green, jade green suits and dresses. Wear any color that is rich and subtle: salmon, ivory, beige, taupe, pewter, paprika, deep peach, and bronze for blouses and accents.

Avoid: Pure white, any bright electric color which will be overpowering and black and white combinations. Mix black with a light soft color such as ivory, jade or peach.

Now that you know your color category and the basic colors for your business wardrobe, you may be finding it difficult to visualize some colors from your list. For example, what is the difference between a true red, a warm or yellow red and a blue red? Or, what is a blue-green or emerald turquoise? Help is at hand. You can order a color swatch wallet of corporate colors for your color category by calling the Image Resource Group. See appendix for phone number or order form.

Besides the colors included in your category, there are Universal Colors. These colors can be worn by anyone regardless of his or her coloring because they are not too dark, too light, too bright or too subtle. They also have a balance between warm (yellow) and cool (blue) undertones which complements all skin tones. You will find a list of these colors on page 181 in the chapter on "Selecting Uniforms."

PROFESSIONAL
DRESS FOR MEN
IN HOSPITALITY

"*It* used to be easier!" some men lament as they face their closet each morning or the equally scary scene of a clothing store, with so many choices that they don't know where to start. For most men, shopping for clothes is akin to visiting a psychologist and having to take a Rorschach test. Or, as James Morgan, a writer for the *Washington Post Magazine,* says: *"You go into a little room, stare at yourself in a mirror and decide who you want to be."*

Like most men, many male hospitality professionals dislike shopping for clothes because they dislike making mistakes and buying business clothing is one area which comes without instructions. In fact, many men don't even feel comfortable talking about it. In this section we will walk you from the clothing store to your closet and then to your work place and out into the business world. You will find guidelines to help you select and wear your business wardrobe with ease and confidence. Once you master the seemingly mysterious *world of clothing,* you will be able to choose and wear clothes with flair that send a message of professionalism and excellence. As we mentioned before, working in hospitality gives you more creative alternatives in attire than many other professions. In addition, you will save time and money and have fun in the process. With this promise in mind, let's begin with a question-naire that will focus on some clothing essentials necessary for being a *well-dressed hospitality professional*.

YOUR CLOTHING IQ

Answer each question with a "Yes" or "No." If your answer is "No", then also answer "Why." You will find the correct answers in the following pages. If you prefer to know the answers right away, you will find them in the back of the book.

1. Is it appropriate to wear a navy-gray, one-sixth-inch pin-striped suit; white shirt; gray and teal, one-inch striped tie and black lace-up shoes for a staff meeting?

Yes _____ No _____ Why? _____

_____

_____

2. Is it appropriate to wear a solid navy suit, light blue shirt, red braces and blue and red foulard tie with matching pocket square for a meeting with a client?

Yes _____ No _____ Why? _____

_____

_____

3. Is it appropriate to wear a black suit, white and gray striped shirt, gray braces and turquoise tie with a white and black paisley pattern for a meeting in which you need to look powerful?

Yes _____ No _____ Why? _____

_____

_____

4. Is it appropriate to wear a brown tweed suit, white oxford shirt, woven yellow pin-dot tie with a clip and cordovan slip-on shoes for a regular workday?

Yes _____ No _____ Why? _____

_____

_____

5. Is it appropriate to wear a gray flannel suit, a white button-down short-sleeved shirt, geometric tie and loafer shoes with buckles for an ordinary day at work?

Yes _____ No _____ Why? _____

_____

_____

6. If you work at a resort property, is it appropriate to wear an olive tweed sport coat with beige pants, a striped white and olive button-down shirt with a medallion tie and brown slip-on shoes for a regular workday?

Yes _____ No _____ Why? _____

_____

_____

7. Is it appropriate to wear a dark gray suit, white tone-on-tone shirt with French cuffs, gold cuff links and a light silver and black woven micro-patterned tie with a black-and-white pocket square to a cocktail party with some of your clients?

Yes _____ No _____ Why? _____

_____

_____

8. Is it appropriate to wear a subtly patterned navy suit, blue and white striped shirt and burgundy and white medium-size dot tie for a meeting at which you will be making a presentation?

Yes _____ No _____ Why? _____

_____

_____

THE PERFECT SUIT

Fortunately in the '90s, men's suits are comfortable and subtly tailored without the stuffy look of the past. Throughout history, men's suits have only slowly changed shapes, lapels, vents and buttons. The latest move toward comfort is just another element in the menswear evolution, a change enthusiastically welcomed by businessmen. Despite the revolutionary changes in fashion and all the

Your suits are the
most important
part of your
wardrobe.

publicity predicting the demise of the suit from a man's wardrobe, experts believe that the traditional suit, in its current form, will survive another 50 years. Having taken years to arrive, the softened suit is here to stay.

"A perfect suit is like money in the bank. It is always there when you need it, always ready and always right," says Lois Fenton, author of *Dress for Excellence.* Your suits are the most important part of your wardrobe. As you move toward excellence, you may find that 60 to 70 percent of your clothing budget will go for suits. They are the most expensive items in your wardrobe and will last a long time if properly cared for. The quality and fit of the suit also says a lot about you. In a world that operates on first impressions, the quality of the suit is often taken as a measure of the man himself. Therefore choosing, buying and wearing a suit takes some planning.

"Eighty percent of the price of a suit is determined by two main elements: the fabric and the amount of hand workmanship that goes into its tailoring," says Kenneth Karpinski, author of *Red Socks Don't Work.* Let's examine the type of fabric, the silhouette and the tailoring details that will comprise the perfect suit for you.

FABRICS

Quality garments are made from one of two fabrics—either *natural* fibers such as wool, cotton, silk, camel hair and cashmere or *blends of natural or manmade fibers* such as 55% wool/45% polyester; 95% wool/5% Alpaca, and so forth. Wool is considered nature's miracle fiber. Wool absorbs moisture, it provides superior comfort in both hot and cold weather and it's durable. A wool fiber can be bent more than 20,000 times without breaking. By comparison, cotton breaks after 3,200 bends and viscose rayon breaks after only 75 bends. Wool also has a natural "memory"—after each stretching, it returns to its original shape. And, as an added bonus, because wool is antistatic it does not attract soil easily. Wool is the all-around best choice for your business suits.

WORSTED WOOL is a lightweight wool made of fine, tightly woven threads that give the fabric a smooth, firm feel. Worsted wears well and falls into a soft drape; its tight weave helps hold the shape of a suit as well as the crease in trousers. Worsted is a good choice for a year-round suit because it offers the advantages of wool without a heavy "wintery" look.

WOOLENS are another breed of wool, made of loosely woven yarns that create a soft textile such as Harris tweed or flannel. Their use is essentially limited to cool winter months.

BLENDS can be made up of natural fibers or natural and manmade such as polyester or acrylic. The recommended blend is 55% wool and 45% polyester or a similar proportion with at least 55% wool. A blend needs little care and wears well; creases stay creased longer than pure wool and wrinkles drop out easier. A blend is less expensive than 100% wool unless it has silk in it, such as wool-silk blends.

A pure polyester suit will not measure up to a professional look. The fabric does not breathe and when the weather gets hot it will feel like you're wearing a sauna. In addition, its shiny look will broadcast poor quality even across a crowded room.

Most of your business suits will be pure wool and some wool blends, especially if your job requires travel. To test the quality of the fabric, read the label on the suit's sleeve for fiber content and "scrunch" up the fabric in your hand. Note how it feels—smooth or rough? Does it wrinkle easily? Do the wrinkles remain after you release the fabric or does it quickly conform to its original shape? Suits made with quality fabrics are a smart investment that pay off in comfort and appearance.

PATTERNS

Pattern is another element that affects the formality and appropriateness of a suit. The pattern plus the cut of the suit, which we will discuss next, also affects the way your suit complements your body structure. The patterns that are considered appropriate for business are subtle, which means you can distinguish the pattern close-up but it looks like a solid from a distance. Following are some of the more common patterns.

SOLID

The most popular and versatile of all "patterns." A solid is easy to combine with shirts and ties and can be dressy or less dressy depending on the intensity of the color. The darker the color, the dressier the suit. Solid suits in navy and gray in the right shade for your coloring and in the right cut for your body shape, are the foundation of your business wardrobe. They are accepted in any business situation.

PINSTRIPE

A fine line, or stripe, either solid or broken, running vertically through the suit. The wider the space between the stripes, the dressier the suit is. If you have broad shoulders, select wide-spaced stripes. For a smaller frame, narrow-spaced stripes are more complementary.

CHALK STRIPES

Wider stripes that look like they were drawn with a piece of chalk. This stripe is dressier than pinstripes and more conservative. Contrary to common belief, wide-spaced, thicker stripes have a slimming effect on a person with a broad or heavy body structure.

HERRINGBONE

This is a weave in a chevron-like design similar to the skeleton of a fish. Now available in lightweight fabrics, it is a dressy suit that adds variety to your wardrobe. It complements all body types.

GLEN PLAID

Also called a glen check, this is a traditional English/Scottish design. It has white and black threads with an over-plaid in another shade or color. It is a less dressy suit, very appropriate for all body types especially if the colors are blended.

HOUNDSTOOTH

A check design which resembles the tooth of a dog. The pattern size will be micro for suits and larger for sport coats. It is less dressy than a glen plaid, and it may be worn by all body types since it looks like a solid from a distance.

WINDOWPANE

A box weave of a thin pencil line usually woven in over a plaid, check, herringbone, twill and sometimes a solid. This pattern is less dressy and looks best on a person with regular to wide shoulders and body frame.

STYLE

All suits will be a variation of one of the following four basic styles or *silhouettes*. Silhouette is the term that the clothing industry uses to describe the cut or shape of a suit. Today the four basic silhouettes are: Sack Suit, European Cut, Updated and Athletic Cut. You will choose the cut that best fits and complements your body type. Study the characteristics of each style and try them on; the correct cut for you should be readily apparent after you have done your homework.

THE SACK. Also called the Brooks Brothers Natural Shoulder, this suit has been a traditional classic American design

THE SACK

THE
EUROPEAN CUT

THE UPDATED
AMERICAN

THE
ATHLETIC CUT

for almost 100 years. It has a shapeless, non-darted jacket with narrow unpadded shoulders with flap pockets, a single rear vent and a two-button front. Men with square or full bodies enjoy the comfort of this boxy, ample shape.

THE EUROPEAN CUT. This suit has a jacket with squarish shoulders, high armholes and a tight fit through the chest and hips. It is two- or three-buttoned, its back is usually non-vented and it has a much more structured feel to it than any other cut. The trousers tend to have a lower rise and fit more snugly through the buttocks and thigh, sitting just under the waist. Its intent is to produce a slim, trim look. Since the jacket is ventless, the person who wears it must unbutton it when sitting down. This cut is best on men with a thin, tall body with narrow hips and a flat bottom.

THE UPDATED AMERICAN CUT. This is a combination of the best elements of the Sack and the European-cut suit. The jacket is tapered at the waist, giving the wearer a V-shape appearance. Depending on the fashion trend, it may have a side, center vent or no vent at all. If you prefer, you can ask the clothier to close the side or center vent for a more tapered silhouette. The shoulders may be padded and the jacket shape will conform to current fashion trends. This suit complements most body types giving the option for elegance, practicality and flair.

THE ATHLETIC CUT. With the emphasis on fitness, this cut is becoming more popular especially on the west coast. This cut has a drop—the distance between the chest and the waist—of eight to ten inches. It is cut with larger shoulders and thighs, making it perfect for the body builder-type who could not fit into any other cut.

THE DOUBLE-BREASTED SUIT— IS IT FOR YOU?

There is a popular misconception about who can wear a double-breasted suit. The double-breasted jacket has been recommended only for tall men that have a trim figure. The reality is that almost anyone can wear a double-breasted jacket and look sharp as long as the jacket is cut properly. One of the few exceptions will be the person with extremely broad hips. One of the advantages of the double-breasted suit—especially for the shorter man—is that the peaked lapel forms an uninterrupted line when the jacket is buttoned on the lower button. The diagonal line across the body can make him look taller.

The double-breasted suit, with the exception of the shawl-collared dinner jacket, should always have peaked lapels; it can be double vented or not vented. It usually has six buttons on the front of the coat, one or two of which can actually be buttoned. It is usually called "six on one" or "six on two" by the clothiers. Trousers tend to be double- or triple-pleated with one-and-one-half-inch cuffs to keep the bottoms properly weighted for a crisp silhouette. If you elect to wear a double-breasted jacket, *you must keep the jacket buttoned,* except when sitting down. You have a choice of either buttoning the bottom button or the middle button, but never both. Buttoning only the bottom button gives you a longer line and especially flatters the shorter man.

Contrary to popular misconception, almost anyone (the exception being someone with extremely broad hips) can wear a double-breasted jacket and look sharp as long as the jacket is cut properly. One of the advantages of the double-breasted suit—especially for the shorter man—is that the uninterrupted line of the peaked lapel when buttoned on the lower button can make a man look taller, as it cuts diagonally across the body. On the other hand, buttoning the middle or waist button can break up the length of a tall man, balancing his stature better.

The double-breasted suit became popular in the '80s; it is still accepted in the '90s as a standard suit in a man's wardrobe, not as a fashion statement, says Steven J. Barnett, a clothing expert. He says that even the most conservative dressers now wear the double-breasted suit. Therefore, when planning your wardrobe, include single- and double-breasted suits. (When selecting single-breasted suits, choose a three-button style. Steven predicts that the three-button suit for both business and leisure wear will be, over the next decade, the best seller.)

VEST OR NO VEST?

As this book was being readied for publication, the vest was making a comeback. In the summer of 1994, *USA Today* published an article announcing that several men's clothing manufacturers were launching their first collection of three-piece traditional vented suits. You will see vests with or without lapels, and you will be able to combine patterned vests with sport coats. Remember if you choose to wear a vest, always leave the last button unbuttoned. For a hospitality professional who spends a lot of his time away from his desk—sometimes even needing to roll up his sleeves to assist in moving chairs, boxes and so forth—wearing a vest is an advantage since it raises the dressiness of just a shirt and tie.

TROUSERS

Trousers are cut in two styles: plain front and pleated front. Pleated pants combine function and comfort, resulting in fewer wrinkles, more circulation and they flatter any figure. "Eighty percent of the trousers today are pleated," says Ken Karpinski, a men's clothing expert. In fitting pleated trousers, the key is to have enough fullness in the thigh so the pleat does not pull open when you are standing. Traditionally, the width of the bottom of a man's trousers was cut to balance the size of his shoe. This means that the width should be up to three-quarters of the length of the shoe. This is the reason why the line of the trouser is slightly tapered. Cuffed trousers have a straight hem and the bottom of the cuff should break slightly over your instep. On uncuffed trousers, the slanted hem should fall lower at the back of the shoe—your tailor will know exactly where. You can judge the proper length of your trousers by taking a little stroll. If your socks do not show as you walk, your trousers are long enough.

The reason for cuffs today is that with lightweight fabrics they give more weight and "hang" to the trousers, emphasizing the line for a neater appearance, especially for trousers with pleats. If you are tall, your cuffs should be one-and-one-half inches; if you are short, one-and-a quarter inch cuffs will give your trousers the appropriate look.

THE PERFECT SUIT THAT FITS

Now that you have made the main decisions about your suit—fabric, pattern and style—it is time to look at proper fit, which is just as important as the fabric and cut you have selected. Going from top to bottom, there are nine areas to check for proper fit when trying on a new suit and to recheck after many wearings to ensure that the fit is still correct.

1 The jacket collar should hug the back of your neck, without gaping or standing away. It should lay smoothly against your shirt collar, exposing about one-half-inch of shirt. If you need alterations to eliminate horizontal ridges of fabric or creases below the collar, select another jacket since alterations of this kind are expensive and difficult.

2 When trying on a jacket, make sure that the shoulder and armhole fit comfortably and that you have enough space to move your arms. If the jacket has little shoulder padding, the seam where the sleeve is joined to the jacket shoulder should extend slightly beyond your own shoulder. With a European cut that has more shoulder padding, the extension will be greater.

3 The front of the jacket is one of the more visible parts of your suit, so it must fit properly. When the coat is buttoned, the lapels should lay smoothly against your chest without wrinkles or bubbles. If the lapels bow out, the jacket is too small for you.

4 When the coat is buttoned, you should have a slight definition at the waist, but not sharply defined like an hourglass. The top button on a two-button jacket should lay approximately at your natural waist.

5 The back of your jacket should fall without creating any creases. It should hug the hips and gently follow the curve of your lower back. Horizontal creases mean that the jacket is too tight; vertical creases mean the jacket is too large. The non-vented jacket hugs the hips with a cleaner line; the center vent maintains a clean line at the hip (unlike side vents) with relative freedom to move. Depending on the fabric, the jacket could be let out or taken in at the center seam.

The jacket should cover the curvature of your seat completely, extending one to one-and-one-half inches below the seat of your trousers. Shorter legs call for a shorter jacket and vice-versa. Your tailor and a mirror are the best advisers here.

6 The sleeves of the jacket should reach the point where your hand meets your wrist, allowing the shirt cuff to extend about one-half inch beyond. The correct measurement is taken while standing with your arms naturally at your side. Always have both sleeves measured since your arms may be different lengths.

7 Suit trousers should fit at the waist, not at the hips. They should be cut to drape from the rear, rather than to cling to the body. Always wear trousers at your navel. The trouser creases should be clearly visible from the bottom portion of the side pocket all the way down. Trousers should be worn wide enough across the hips so that there is no pulling across the front pockets (allowing easy hand entry), and the pockets should remain smoothly closed when not in use. With pleated trousers, the pleats should not spread apart when you are standing straight.

8 Trouser bottoms should break at the instep of your shoes. A slight, medium, or full break at the shoe is a personal style and comfort choice. Cuffs that measure about one-and-one-half inches give more weight and pull, emphasizing the line of the trousers and acting as an anchor to help the pants drape properly.

QUALITY DETAILS

When purchasing a suit, look for the details that give the garment quality and comfort. Some of the most important details are invisible and involve the construction of the garment. A good suit is partially handmade. No machine can duplicate the hand tailoring that makes a suit look and feel high quality. The latest technologies allow some of the tailoring tasks—such as buttonholes and hemlines—to be done by machine with almost similar results. But a garment that is handstitched allows the tailor to adjust the garment to suit your comfort needs.

It is important to check the following details:

COLLAR. A hand-sewn collar is more rounded and, therefore, lies flat against the neck. A machine-sewn collar is straighter and does not follow the curve of the neck as well; this is especially noticeable when you are seated.

PATTERNS. Stripes, plaids and other patterns should match at the critical points: the lapels, back seam, pockets and seat of the pants.

BUTTONS. The best buttons are made from horn and sewn by hand. Plastic buttons break easily with dry cleaning.

JACKET CHEST PIECE. This is the piece that goes between the fabric and the lining to give the coat its shape. If you can separate the lining from the suiting fabric, the piece has probably been fused or glued. This sometimes makes the suit look stiff and shortens its life since the stiff fabric will pucker out. Now, with better technology, the fusing process is done with more resistance to heat and pressing. When this piece is sewn instead of fused it is a sign of quality which will be reflected in the price tag of the suit. A sewn piece is very soft and keeps the shape of the jacket, molding it to your body; it also is not damaged by dry cleaning.

BLAZERS/SPORT JACKETS

Even though a suit is considered the proper business look for men who work at most city and some resort properties, there are some properties, especially in smaller towns and most resorts, in which a sport coat is not only an option, but probably the required dress for those employees not in uniform. For those who wear suits most of the time, the sport coat gives a smart dressed-down look for those relaxed social occasions that are conducted away from the office.

Blazers are jackets in solid colors and sport coats are jackets in a patterned fabric. The appropriate colors for blazers are navy, gray, camel, taupe, olive, pine and burgundy. Choose a color for your blazer that complements your coloring. The navy blazer is probably one of the most appropriate items that you can have in your business wardrobe; it is considered a classic, is easy to combine and you can wear it year round for both business and social occasions. The navy blazer is also an example of how differently men and women can perceive the world: Most women hate to walk into a social gathering and find another woman wearing the same outfit; most men panic if they don't see 12 other men wearing exactly the same thing they've got on—which is usually the navy blazer!

The patterns for sport coats can be bolder than the ones suggested for suits, including herringbone, tweeds, subtle plaids and houndstooth. You also have more fabric options for sport coats: wools, worsted wool, cashmere, linen and wool blends and silk and silk blends, the latter two being especially cool options for warm weather. The most elegant look when wearing a sport coat is to keep the bottom of your outfit simple: solid taupe, gray, light to medium gray, khaki or beige trousers are the best options when wearing both blazers and sport coats. Avoid patterned trousers. Wear your chosen combinations of pattern and colors near your face with your jacket, shirt and tie.

The style and fit of a well-cut sport jacket closely follows that of the suit jacket. However, a sport coat should fit you a little looser to accommodate a sweater or vest. The sport jacket also has some non-suit details such as brass buttons, the swelled edges on the lapels and patch pockets. Avoid leather or suede elbow patches since they are too casual for business. The double-breasted blazer is dressier than the single-breasted, but both are still more casual and relaxed than the suit.

THE SHIRT

According to *The Shirt Report,* which is published by the Shirt Store in New York City, the average businessman will spend approximately 100,000 hours in a dress shirt and will buy at least 500 of them at a cost of $20,000 during his career. For such an important companion, you want to be sure that it is enhancing your professional image. Gone are the days when blue and discreet stripes were the only shirt options for the businessman. Today there are many choices in fabric, styles and colors; selecting carefully will ensure both professionalism and comfort.

Let's examine the fabric, color, collar, cuffs and fit—all elements that should be considered when purchasing a shirt.

FABRIC. "The shirt is the piece of clothing that is closest to your body; it needs to act almost like your second skin and cotton performs this function the best," says Alan Flusser, author of *Clothes and the Man.* Fine-quality dress shirts are made of 100 percent cotton. Cotton "breathes" and absorbs moisture which allows the body to cool itself. Another option is cotton blends that are at least 60 percent cotton. Depending on the weave and the finish, the fabric makes the shirt dressy or casual. The two basic weaves are the *broadcloth* which is smooth and has a silky finish appropriate for a dress shirt and the *oxford* which has a rougher finish and is used in a button-down style. Wearing an oxford shirt with a navy striped or solid suit sends a mixed signal—the suit is dressy and the shirt is more casual. The oxford shirt, however, is a good complement to a blazer or sport coat. (Read "From Dressy to Casual" on page 45 for a complete comparison of suits, shirts and ties.)

PINPOINT OXFORD is similar to oxford but is made from a much finer yarn; it is more tightly woven which gives the fabric a smoother, silkier and, hence, dressier look. It falls in between the broadcloth and the oxford in terms of dressiness. *End-on-end* is in a similar category as the pinpoint; one weave runs white threads in one direction and blue or pink in the other. The best fabrics on the market are the *Egyptian* and *Sea Island* cottons, which are finer, tighter and feel like silk to the touch. *Tone-on-tone* is a design that uses two or more tones of the same color giving the fabric a shiny effect; it is used for very dressy shirts.

COLOR. When conducting a seminar for a large city hotel in the early 1980s, the general manager took me aside before the session and told me that in his hotel only white and blue shirts were allowed. Today you have more options for shirt colors. Choose some of the pastel shades listed in your color category to create a different look appropriate to the occasion. Colored shirts make you look more approachable. When the pastel shade looks almost white with just a tint of color, it makes the shirt dressier. White and soft white shirts will give you a dressier and more authoritative look. Changing your pure white shirt for a pale blue one will tone down the power look of your dark navy suit. The darker the color of your shirt, the less dressy it becomes. If you wear sport coats

Rectangular-Square Jaw

Avoids
• long points

Standard collar

Average to slightly short collar

Average to slightly wide spread

Button down

Pin collar

Tab collar

Square

Avoids
• wide and short collars

Standard collar

Average to slightly long collars

Average to slightly narrow spread

Pin collar

Button down

Tab collar

Inverted Triangle   **Diamond**

Avoids
- long points
- pin collar
- Button down

Standard collar   Slightly short collar   Average to slightly spread collar

---

Oval   **Oblong**

Avoids
- long points
- round collar

Standard collar   Slightly wide spread   Short length

Button down

Round

Avoids
- round collar
- narrow spread
- long points

Slightly wide spread   Slightly short collar   Button down

and blazers to work, you will have more freedom to experiment with colors; try deep mauve, periwinkle, jade green, beige, deep green and deep peach.

There are options besides solid shirts. We invite our seminar participants to "Go ahead—dare to be striped." If you desire a conservative look, choose shirts with narrow stripes of one color on a crisp white background. Try any of the three types of stripes: the pin (smallest), the pencil or the candy stripe (one-eighth inch). Stripes on a white background are more dressy such as a white shirt with burgundy or navy stripes. White stripes on a color background are less dressy such as a blue shirt with white or gray stripes.

COLLAR. Since the shirt is the closest clothing item to your face, it must complement your physical proportions. You want to look for balance. For example, if your face is broad and your neck is thick, a tiny collar will look out of balance. At the same time, a shirt with long points will overwhelm a small man with delicate features. There are two things to consider when selecting the right collar style: the *spread* relates to the distance between the points of the collar which can be narrow, medium or wide; and the *points length* which can be short, average or long. For balance, follow this chart to select the best shirt collar for your face shape.

See "From Dressy to Casual" on page 45 for dressy shirt collar styles.

There should be a balance between the shirt collar and the tie. For a standard collar and a button-down collar, the half-Windsor knot or the four-in hand are the preferred choice. The tab collar needs a tighter four-in hand knot and a wide spread collar looks balanced with a half-or full-Windsor knot. With the new woven tie fabrics, the four-in-hand knot is the most recommended for all shirt collars.

A note on quality: a fine collar is always stitched around the edges to stiffen and hold the folded material in place. The stitches should be in a single row and not more than one-quarter inch from the collar edge. The finer the shirt, the finer the stitching.

CUFFS. Shirt cuffs are another element to consider when selecting shirts. The two basic styles are the single or barrel cuff, with one or two buttons, and the double or French cuff. French cuffs are dressier and the required cuff links let you express your personality. For the most elegant look, select simple, small-sized gold or silver, mother-of-pearl or matte finish stone like onyx. If you choose metal it should match the metal of your watch: silver-toned with a silver watch and gold-toned with a gold watch. If you don't want the added investment of cuff links, try a pair of simple, colorful silk knots.

FIT. When choosing a shirt, it is very important that it fit right.

A study conducted by Cornell University found that nearly 70 percent of businessmen were wearing their collars too tight. The reality is that shirts shrink and necks thicken. When buttoned, the collar should be loose enough to comfortably insert one finger between your neck and the collar. If you can't do this, not only will you be uncomfortable but your tie won't sit properly and the points of the shirt will not lay correctly. On the other hand, if the shirt is too large, it is equally unprofessional. If you have a problem with your neck size, consider investing in custom-made shirts. It would be a wise choice since the shirt is framing your face.

Also remember that your cuff should extend one-fourth inch below the jacket if you wear a single cuff and one-half inch below for double cuffs. Showing no cuff or wearing short sleeves with suits is not acceptable, regardless of the weather. The "guayavera," worn on many islands, is the only short-sleeve overshirt that is appropriate for social and public functions if worn by the local businessmen. Otherwise, even in the islands, your regular long-sleeve shirt is the required business look.

More and more men are having their ready-to-wear shirts monogrammed with two or three initials. Keep your monogram as understated as possible. A monogram on the collar or the cuff invites too much attention. If the shirt has a pocket, center your initials on it. If the shirt lacks a pocket, as many custom-made shirts do, have the monogram placed approximately five or six inches up from the waist, centered on the left side of the shirt. And please use your own initials, not the shirt designer's; after all you own the shirt, not him!

TIES—YOUR PERSONAL SIGNATURE

Without performing any apparent function, your tie is, perhaps, the one item of your attire that reveals the most about you. Your tie is your *personal signature;* it gives you an opportunity for self-expression, individuality and distinctiveness. Your tie is usually the most colorful of all the clothes you wear in business and it is the one item that people remember. In addition, the tie literally ties together the entire look of a well-dressed man. Therefore, it is the one clothing item that you should select yourself; you may welcome an opinion from your significant other, but be sure that you make the final selection.

Silk is the basic fabric in all fine neckties because it takes the dye and holds a knot better. The quality and weight of the silk, the interlining and the slipstitching which connects the tie together, all give a tie its distinction.

Silk neckties come in two basic styles—smooth and ribbed. *Smooth silk,* often called foulard silk, has a smooth finish and is relatively lightweight. It includes the printed silks which come in different patterns from dots and geometrics to florals and conversational. *Ribbed or woven silk,* usually much heavier, includes several classifications such as repp silk (used in regimental striped ties), faille silk (used in club ties), raw silk and crepe de Chine (used in dressy ties). Don't waste your money on synthetic ties; they do not hold a knot well, and they do not look as good or have the luxurious feel of the natural fabrics.

Fish ties do not swim in corporate waters

At a major hotel convention that I attended a few years ago, one of the topics discussed at my dinner table was the fish tie that one of the speakers wore to his workshop; we did not discuss his presentation. He might have intended to be humorous, but his credibility suffered. When selecting ties, the fabric and pattern determine its appropriateness for a particular occasion. The general guideline: Woven silk ties are dressier than printed silk ties; they have a softer hand and are generally richer looking than the printed ones. For the printed ties, the shiny fabrics such as satin are dressier and more appropriate for evening wear.

The size of the pattern also affects the level of dressiness, and the rule is the smaller the pattern, the dressier the tie. In the late 1980s, the size and type of tie patterns ran amok. During this same time, one corporate president hired me to meet with his managers from all over the country at a seminar on the west coast. This president said, "I'm tired of seeing them wear those wild ties with birds and large flowers. I'm getting comments and negative remarks from our clients." The great variety of tie choices had created grand confusion for business men. Today you have even more variety and, therefore, more room to make mistakes. Yes, the size of the tie patterns did grow larger in the 1980s. In the 1990s the pattern size is much smaller—almost micro—but it will take a few more years for this trend to appear in all stores and clothing catalogs. Two of these dressy micro patterns are the *Macclesfield,* an open weave with a geometric design in contrasting tones such as gray and burgundy, and the *Grenadine,* a thin, loosely woven lightweight silk with an almost irregular surface and a design so tiny that it is considered almost a solid.

When selecting tie patterns for business, choose any pattern that has a *name,* such as: repp-tie, foulard, dot, solid or paisley for a conservative look. Select the new patterns such as medallion (or a larger foulard), abstract or geometric for a less conservative but still professional look with some flair. You will always be safe if the size of the pattern is no larger than a quarter. A pattern the size of two quarters is appropriate for the office if the colors are blended. Going beyond the pattern size of three quarters for a tie with bright colors during the daytime is risky business. Abstracts in subtle colors could be large because from a distance they will look like solids. Avoid birds, faces, turtles, giraffes—anything representational of something that moves or is alive. These are called "conversational" ties and along with florals, faces and cartoon characters should be used for casual events or in the evening only.

When wild ties were popular in the late '80s, John Molloy, the author of *Dress for Success,* took pictures of men wearing traditional shirts and ties with wild patterns. He showed them to a cross-

Ties end at belt line.

section of the business community, and asked what they thought these men did for a living. Over 90 percent of the respondents thought the men in wild ties were executives and professionals. But when he ran the same experiment at the end of 1993 with new wild ties, 24 percent of the men were described as "blue collar." The best way to be certain your ties are up-to-date and to foresee the trends, is to go to the most exclusive men's store in your area and ask the salesperson to show you some of the most expensive ties. These ties will be an example of the latest trend which will take about a year to come to other manufacturers at more moderate prices.

The width of the tie should balance the lapels of the suit. To be sure your tie is in balance, hold the wide end of your tie up against the widest part of the jacket lapel. The tie should not be wider than the lapel. It can be narrower, but not too much. Tie widths change every four to five years and the change is measured only in millimeters. Keeping up with the trend is easy and, likewise, it is easy for everyone to notice that you are wearing your old ties!

Make sure your tie stops at the top of your belt line; forego tie clips and tie tacks (the clips are too old fashioned and the tie tack will make a hole in your wonderful tie!). Many hospitality professionals, especially those who work in food and beverage, use tie clips because otherwise their ties dip into food and drinks. The updated solution to this problem is to buy the tie accessory that invisibly holds your tie in place by attaching the tie's label loop to the shirt through a buttonhole. Ask the salesperson for it; it will solve your problem without distracting from your personal signature!

Another option to keep your tie in place is what is called The Tie Trap. It is a five-inch long piece of ribbon with two buttonholes on either end. You attach one end of the ribbon to your fourth shirt button, thread the ribbon through the tie label and attach the other end to the fifth shirt button. It is manufactured by a company in Illinois. (See appendix for phone number)

POCKET HANDKERCHIEFS

A pocket handkerchief, known also as a pocket square, can add a touch of flair to your business look. If you choose to wear one, select silk in a color that coordinates with your tie but does not match it exactly. A tie that exactly matches a pocket square sends a message that the wearer lacks creativity! The easiest way to select a handkerchief is to wear a plain color in one of the dominant colors from your tie. Selecting a different pattern could be more interesting; for example, a paisley pocket square with a foulard or a geometric tie would give your suit pizzazz. The latest version of a linen pocket square trimmed in navy, black or burgundy can be quite dashing. The pocket square gives your suit or sport coat a dressy touch.

PUTTING THEM ALL TOGETHER
COMBINING JACKETS, SHIRTS AND TIES

Among the most common clothing questions men ask their spouses is: "Does this tie go with this suit?" Or, "Is this shirt good with this suit?" One executive from a large hotel who is always impeccably dressed confessed to me that before each trip his wife puts small white stickers with numbers on his clothes so he will coordinate her combinations correctly. He is right to care about such detail. The tasteful coordination of jacket, shirt and tie not only makes you look good, it shows your sense of creativity and organization. People assume that you will bring those same qualities to your job.

Here is the key of how to do it: The formula for excellent clothing coordination is to coordinate the fabric, pattern, color and dressiness of the items in your outfit.

COMPARABLE FABRICS

The texture and the finish of the fabrics should be similar; this makes the outfit balanced with the same level of dressiness. For example, a worsted wool suit with a broadcloth shirt and fine silk tie; all of these have a smooth texture giving the outfit a dressy look. On the other hand, a glen plaid tweed sport coat, an oxford shirt and a knit wool tie all have more texture giving the outfit a casual look. Shiny fabrics are more dressy and matte-finish fabrics are more casual.

COMBINING COLORS

- *Your shirt should be lighter than your suit.* Dress shirts are usually in light colors ranging from white to light gray to pastels; these create contrast when mixed with dark suits. Example: A blue-gray suit with a light blue shirt or a navy suit with a light gray shirt. A shirt darker than the jacket is appropriate for sport coats only; this combination makes the outfit more casual. Example: A deep blue shirt with a camel jacket.
- *Your tie should be darker than your shirt.* Lack of contrast can result in a dull monochromatic look. The tie should stand out from the shirt background as a focal point.
- *Your tie repeats the color of the suit, the color of the shirt or both.* When we say repeat, it does not mean exactly the same shade, but the *same color family.* Example: Pair a gray suit with a teal and rust pattern, a light gray shirt and a tie in teal, gray and yellow foulard. The shade of gray in the suit, shirt and tie would be different, but the gray color is what *ties* the three items together.

Men's clothing expert Ken Karpinski has detailed the four steps to combine colors: Identify, Isolate, Amplify and Coordinate. Based on his concept let's go through the process of putting colors together following these steps:

1. IDENTIFY: Look carefully at your suit and find the colors in the fabric; you will be surprised at how many colors are woven in, especially if you are looking at a patterned suit. You will find accent stripes, color nubs and slubs. For example, consider a subtle glen plaid gray suit; let's say the overall look of the suit is gray but up close we find it has very fine lines in teal, burgundy and blue.

2. ISOLATE: Decide which color you want to "pull out." In our example, we will isolate burgundy.

3. AMPLIFY: Once you have determined the color, you need to

FROM DRESSY TO CASUAL

The following chart will help you select the jacket, shirt and tie within the same level of dressiness.

Keep dressy with dressy (a.a)
Combine dressy with less dressy (a.b.)
Combine less dressy with casual(b.c)
Do not combine dressy with casual;
Do not wear a double-breasted suit with a button-down shirt.

SUITS-SPORT COATS

a. Dressy:
solid dark color
pinstripe
shiny fabric
double-breasted
black suit—evening only

b. Less Dressy:
herringbone
glen plaid
subtle pattern
windowpane
fine tweed
silk blends

c. Casual:
houndstooth
tweed
bold plaid
linen-silk blends

SHIRTS

a. Dressy:
Sea Island/Egyptian cotton
tone-on-tone
broadcloth
solid white
contrasting white collar
spread collar
standard collar
solid icy colors—almost white

b. Less Dressy:
pinpoint
end-on-end
stripes on white background
button-down broadcloth
solid pastel colors

c. Casual
stripes on a color background
solid medium colors
checks
tattersall
graph check
plaids

TIES

a. Dressy:
solid silk
woven silk
pin dots
micro patterns
shiny fabrics
white dots on dark background

b. Less Dressy:
foulard
stripes
repp stripe
paisley
medallion
abstracts
geometric
abstract

c. Casual:
club
knit
wool
plaid

Ties

Ties	Solid Suit or Coat	Striped Suit	Herringbone Suit or Coat	Glen Plaid Suit	Subtle Tweed Suit	Houndstooth Coat	Tweed Coat
Solid Silk	• Solid Shirt • Stripes • Plaid* • Tattersall*	• Solid Shirt • Stripes (Different widths)	• Solid Shirt • Stripes • Tattersall* • Plaid*	• Solid Shirt • Stripes • Tattersall*	• Solid Shirt • Stripes		
Pin Dots	• Solid Shirt • Stripes	• Solid Shirt	• Solid Shirt	• Solid Shirt			
Stripes	• Solid Shirt • Stripes (Different widths) • Tattersall*	• Solid Shirt	• Solid Shirt • Tattersall*	• Solid Shirt	• Solid Shirt	• Solid Shirt*	• Solid Shirt*
Foulard	• Solid Shirt • Stripes	• Solid Shirt • Stripes (Different widths)	• Solid Shirt	• Solid Shirt	• Solid Shirt • Stripes	• Solid Shirt*	• Solid Shirt* • Stripes*
Paisley	• Solid Shirt • Stripes • Tattersall*	• Solid Shirt	• Solid Shirt	• Solid Shirt	• Solid Shirt • Stripes	• Solid Shirt*	• Solid Shirt*
Medallion	• Solid Shirt • Stripes	• Solid Shirt • Striped Shirt (Different widths)	• Solid Shirt	• Solid Shirt	• Solid Shirt • Stripes	• Solid Shirt*	• Solid Shirt* • Stripes*
Abstract	• Solid Shirt • Stripes	• Solid Shirt	• Solid Shirt	• Solid Shirt	• Solid Shirt • Stripes	• Solid Shirt*	• Solid Shirt* • Stripes*
Club	• Solid Shirt • Stripes • Tattersall*		• Solid Shirt	• Solid Shirt	• Solid Shirt • Stripes	• Solid Shirt*	• Solid Shirt* • Stripes*
Solid Knit or Wool	• Solid Shirt* • Stripes • Tattersall* • Plaid*		• Solid Shirt*	• Solid Shirt*		• Solid Shirt*	• Solid Shirt* • Stripes* • Plaid* • Tattersall*
Plaid	• Solid Shirt* • Tattersall*		• Solid Shirt*	• Solid Shirt*		• Solid Shirt*	• Solid Shirt*

* For Sport Coat Only

find more of it, and the easiest place to do this is with your tie. Don't try to match the colors perfectly; again, think in terms of color family. Navy, light blue and bright royal blue are from the *blue* family. Burgundy, pink and red are from the *red* family. Teal, green and aqua are from the *green* family.

4. COORDINATE: Now let's take the suit and tie and see how they look together. You may have several candidates picked out, so look for the one that you like the best. For our example let's select a tie with a deep red background with medallions that have blue-green, blue and off-white in the design. Now let's look at three shirts in white, light blue and pink. When looking at the different alternatives, the white shirt looks good if we need a dressier look. For a regular workday, the light blue looks the best. So, the final outfit looks like this: a gray subtle plaid suit with burgundy, teal and blue; a light blue shirt and a medallion tie in deep red with blue-green, blue and off-white. Notice that the burgundy and the deep red are not the same shade but they are in the *same red color family*.

COMBINING PATTERNS

Combine two solids and one pattern. Example: A solid navy suit, white or light blue shirt and striped or foulard tie. Easy!

Combine two patterns and one solid. Example: A striped navy suit, solid blue or white shirt and foulard tie. Using a white shirt makes this combination dressier and fool-proof.

The *lighter the shirt and tie* and the *darker the suit*, the *more formal the look*. For example, a dark charcoal gray suit, white shirt and light grenadine silver tie is dressy.

As you *darken the shirt* and *lighten the color of the tie*, the *outfit becomes more casual*. For example, take a gray patterned suit and pair it with a gray shirt and medium violet with white and yellow foulard tie. The colored shirt makes the outfit more casual. If you want to raise the dressiness of the outfit, change the shirt to a lighter color such as icy gray or white. If you want the outfit to look even dressier, you could change to a deep purple tie.

Combining Three Patterns. In the 1990s, creative hospitality professionals show flair by mixing three patterns. Here's how to correctly combine three patterns:

- The three patterns need to *blend.* One color must be repeated in all three; it can be a different tone but it must be from the same color family.
- Mixing two stripes makes it easier; select them in a *different width* such as a subtle tweed suit, narrow striped shirt and bold striped tie.
- Combine *small* patterns with *bold* patterns such as a herringbone suit, striped shirt and large medallion tie.

BRACES: A COMFORT ISSUE, NOT A FASHION STATEMENT

Trousers were originally made to be worn with *braces,* incorrectly called suspenders. Braces are an item of comfort and a tool for a proper fit. They permit the trousers to hang more neatly than belts allow, supporting the front of the pants as well as the rear. Every man, no matter how thin and trim, has a slight bulge in his stomach area. When the trousers are worn on the waist held by braces, they pass smoothly over this bulge in an even drape. Trousers worn on the hip, however, must be belted tightly, for there is nothing to hold them up. This pressure makes the wearer uncomfortable which causes many men to wear their belts lower than their navel, leaving the stomach area to show above the belt. Some men do not wear braces because they don't want to make a "fashion statement." The first time I got a pair of braces for my husband, he, as a very conservative dresser, did not want to wear anything too "fancy." We discussed the comfort and not the fashion side of braces because for my husband—and many of you men may relate to this—comfortable clothing is the most important element. When he wore his new braces, he, indeed, felt much more comfortable and to his surprise, he looked slimmer! He also received compliments at the office (which also helped). After this positive experience, he decided to wear both his work and casual trousers with braces.

You may remove the trouser loops when your trousers have suspender buttons sewn on; some manufacturers don't even include loops if the garment was designed to be worn without a belt. Even though many Americans do leave the belt loops on when wearing suspenders and many salespersons will approve, it is not the ultimate in taste.

Use only leather button tabs for business and casual wear. Metal clips are used only for jeans or for very casual clothing. The newest looks in suspenders are solids, stripes or patterns in fancy design motifs. Coordinate your braces with the tie and suit without exactly matching either one. A neutral color such as navy, gray or brown-taupe is easy to combine. If you wear leather braces, match your shoes to them. On a day when you choose your boldest tie, put on a more subdued pair of braces. They should not compete with each other for attention. We should not even have to mention that braces are *never* worn with a belt.

BELTS

When selecting belts, anything other than leather in black, brown or cordovan with a simple gold buckle is out of place with a business suit. A belt should be in the same color family as your shoes, although they don't need to match exactly. Avoid showy or decorative belt buckles. You want to draw attention to your face (framed by your shirt, tie and coat combination) not to your waist. The only function of a belt is to hold up your trousers, not to make a statement. Please remember to keep it in good condition!

SHOES

Your professional image of excellence must be complemented by the right shoes and socks. If you want to pick out a well-dressed hospitality professional, look down. Shoes, like ties, say a lot about you and should be the best quality you can afford. In business you have the option of the traditional lace-ups, the capped toe, wing tips or the popular leather slip-on. A laced shoe is dressier. If you choose a slip-on, the simple tassel style is recommended; the so-called penny-loafer is too casual for most business attire including a sport coat. Avoid buckles and boots. In one of our seminars, a front desk manager wore boots. Of course, no one would make him take his boots off; I just explained to him what would happen to his credibility if the guests saw his boots. Boots may be an appropriate shoe in some cities around the country, but the problem is that in hospitality, we are serving guests from all over the world and an item that is traditional to one culture may not be appropriate or understood across the board. In many countries, boots are used only to ride horses.

The most appropriate color for shoes is black combined with black, navy or gray socks. Black shoes go well with all navy and gray suits. Brown shoes are more appropriate with the earth tones, even though some fine clothiers suggest that brown shoes also combine with black, gray and navy. Cordovan—a reddish-black-burgundy (no brown) is another choice for suits and sport coats, especially recommended for slip-ons. Avoid any other color such as navy, gray or light trendy colors. Business shoes should be made only of leather which includes the upper part and the soles. Thick rubber soles, regardless of how comfortable they may be, do not measure up to your professional image. Choose a calfskin leather rather than suede. Remember to coordinate your shoes and belt colors.

CARING FOR YOUR SHOES

"You can tell if a person is meticulous or not by observing whether the shoes are well-cared for, polished or in need of new heels. If they are shabby, then the person is obviously not one who is attentive to details," says men's clothing designer Roger Baugh. Many experts claim that you could double the life of your favorite shoes by simply putting a shoe tree into them at the end of each day. The shoe tree absorbs the moisture produced by daily perspiration which prevents the leather from curling and creasing.

Allow shoes to 'rest' at least 36 to 48 hours after each wearing. Your feet will also benefit, as most podiatrists recommend alternating shoes every day so your feet aren't constantly rubbed at the same points. Polish your shoes after each wearing, removing the dust and surface dirt first; also remember to polish underneath in the arch as well as on the top.

Socks

Choose only wool, cotton, or wool and silk blends. Natural fibers allow a better flow of air, cutting down perspiration and heat, so your feet will remain cool during the day. Select solid colors or subtle patterns such as bird's-eye, nail's head or paisley in colors that blend with the shoe or the trousers. Argyles and bright colors are not appropriate for business; use them for sportswear only. Needless to say, white has no place in business. Regardless of the color and pattern you select, your socks must be long enough to cover the calf. No one would appreciate looking at your hairy leg. This cardinal rule was confirmed by a poll conducted with professional men and women in 1989. The female professionals listed three things about their male colleagues that they considered unprofessional:

- too short socks that allow the leg to show;
- pants below the belly;
- dirty fingernails.

If you want to know what the group of men said about their female colleagues, turn to page 76.

The Finishing Touches

The finishing touches are the accessories that you wear every day that either complement or detract from your image of excellence including your watch, pens and glasses; these should be the best quality you can afford.

Glasses

Many young professionals have discovered that wearing glasses makes them look more credible and authoritative. Many others wear them for practical reasons. Whatever frame you select, the lenses must be clear, not tinted because eye contact is one of the most powerful tools you have in business, and the less interference that you put between you and the other person, the easier the communication process. If your hair and eyebrows are dark, select

dark frames such as tortoise shell. If your hair is light or gray, select a metal frame in either gold or silver.

JEWELRY

When it comes to jewelry, less is more. Here is a simple checklist:

- Limit your rings to two: a signet or similar style and a wedding band.
- Choose a simple and elegant watch with a leather or metal watchband. Avoid plastic, heavy sport watches with calculators or alarms that will interrupt a meeting.
- Leave the disposable pens on your desk. For meetings with clients, peers and supervisors, use a quality ball-point or fountain pen.
- Avoid medallions, gold chains and tribal wood carvings.

The difference between being dressed and well-dressed are the details, and your accessories are the details that are a part of this difference.

A QUICK CHECK BEFORE FACING THE WORLD

Before you leave for work or a social engagement, examine with your best friend—a full length mirror—the overall picture you present and the details from head to toe. Make the necessary changes, add or replace accessories and make sure your appearance and grooming are impeccable. This daily exercise will take just a few minutes but the benefits are worth it. If you can check all the points, you are ready to face the world!

HAIR STYLE

- Short and neat; does not touch shirt collar
- Hair in nose and ears are trimmed
- Mustache well trimmed
- Beard recommended only to cover imperfections

SHIRT
- No wrinkles in collar, cuffs or facing
- Collar loose enough for one finger to fit in neckline
- Collar of shirt stands one-fourth to one-half inches above collar of suit
- Sleeve extends one-eighth to one-fourth inches below the jacket
- No short sleeves with suit jackets

JACKET
- Does not wrinkle across the back
- Length must cover buttocks—measure from collar seam to floor and divide it in half for length
- Collar lies flat against the shirt
- Sleeve length at wrist bone
- Top-stitching is even, no loose threads
- Leather or metal buttons on sport coat only

TIE
- Ends at top of the belt line
- Width matched to lapel width
- No tie tack or clip
- Tie knot is balanced with shirt collar
- Four-in-hand knot for thicker tie fabrics with all collars

JEWELRY
- No bracelets, chains or fancy rings
- No earrings
- No heavy sport watches or calculators
- Simple and elegant are best choices
- Gold, silver or leather watch strap
- Cuff links simple, small size; no fancy or clear stones for day time
- Silver-toned cuff links with silver watch; gold toned with gold watch

TROUSERS

- Just breaking in the front
- If uncuffed, tapered toward the back
- Fall straight from buttocks
- Fit above stomach
- Pockets remain flat, no bulging
- Well pressed

SHOES

- Highly polished
- The best quality you can afford
- Dark color: black, cordovan or brown
- Thin soles
- Tie or slip-on and tassel loafers for suits and sport coats
- Penny loafers or loafers with low vamp for casual wear only
- No boots

SOCKS

- Blend with trousers and shoes
- Subtle patterns that resemble solid from a distance
- Argyles for casual wear only
- Long enough to cover calf; no skin showing

BRIEFCASE

- The best quality you can afford
- Leather only, hard or soft
- No molded plastic or metal
- Discreet combination lock

OTHER ACCESSORIES

- Pocket square that complements tie, never identical to it
- No tinted glasses
- Braces in neutral color, or to complement tie
- No clip-on suspenders for business

- Never wear braces with belt
- Belt color matches shoes
    - no large buckles
    - simple, classic design
    - must be in good condition

PROFESSIONAL DRESS FOR WOMEN IN HOSPITALITY

*I*n today's workplace, women in hospitalty can express both their credibility and their individuality with their business outfits. The times that required a cookie cutter look of a man-tailored suit, shirt, and bow-tie are now gone. This "dress for success" look was necessary 20 years ago. But the times have changed, and today women have proved they can do a so-called man's job without looking like one. Now, professional women's clothing conveys responsibility, position identification, power, and the appearance of competency without looking mannish. In her book *The Power of Dress*, Jacqueline Murray writes "Women finally have a wide variety of choices that work well because they have worked through specific adaptations of the significant male business symbols, and they have established their presence visibly as counterparts as well as equals with their own female position symbols."

However, along with this freedom of choice also comes confusion and uncertainty as to what is appropriate to wear for business. Women are bombarded with conflicting messages about how they should dress for work. Fashion magazines and some department stores display inappropriate career clothing because it appeals to those readers and buyers who want to be on the cutting edge of trendy dressing. Some of the work clothes promoted by these fashion arbiters are inappropriate for most working women. We find pages and pages of models with extremely short and tight outfits that leave professional women wondering how they are supposed to dress for the office. Susie Watson, advertising and public relations director of Timex, Inc., may have said it best: "If I wore to work at my corporation one of the many baby-doll dresses shown by this year's designers, they would think I was sleepwalking!" Too often women hurt themselves in their career by taking too many liberties with their image at work. In hospitality, even though there is room for creativity and flair, your image must convey messages of professionalism and credibility.

Research conducted by the Center for Creative Leadership in North Carolina found that attention to image was vital for women who want to advance in their careers. The overall image of top achieving women was "stylish, sophisticated, businesslike and commanding." As we mentioned before, professional women in hospitality have more creative business attire alternatives. This chapter will provide you with the information to achieve this image of excellence. In this section, we will walk you from the clothing store to your closet and then to your place of work so you will learn the guidelines that will help you select clothes and accessories that send a message of professionalism and credibility, along with the flair that is appropriate in hospitality. With this promise in mind, let's begin with a questionnaire that will focus on some clothing essentials necessary for being a *well-dressed female hospitality professional.*

YOUR CLOTHING IQ

When we think of a well-dressed female hospitality professional, "appropriateness" is a key element that comes to mind. Also, attention to detail in the selection of fabrics, styles, colors, accessories and the art of putting them all together. Answer each question with either "Yes" or "No." If you answer "No" then also answer "Why." You will find all the correct answers in the following pages. If you can't wait, the answers can also be found at the back of the book.

1. During the summer months, is it appropriate to wear a white linen suit, turquoise blouse, black shoes and suntan hose to a staff meeting?

Yes _____ No _____ Why? _____

_____

_____

2. Is it appropriate to wear a navy suit, cream blouse with a high neckline, bone pumps and belt, ivory hose and medium-sized gold earrings to a meeting where you need to look powerful?

Yes _____ No _____ Why? _____

_____

_____

3. Is it appropriate to wear a two-piece, short, elbow length-sleeved dress in a small geometric print of gray, coral and black, with a gray jacket and gray hose and shoes to meet with an executive of your company for an update on a project?

Yes _____ No _____ Why? _____

_____

_____

4. Is it appropriate to wear a flower print silk dress with open neckline, self belt, pearl and gold earrings and sheer hose for a regular day at the office?

Yes _____ No _____ Why? _____

_____

_____

5. Is it appropriate to wear a long-sleeved teal dress, gray pumps with sheer hose and gold dangling earrings for a staff meeting where you will be making a project or work report presentation?

Yes _____ No _____ Why? _____

_____

_____

6. Is it appropriate to wear a red coat dress with a print scarf, a snakeskin gray belt, gray hose and shoes for a regular work day?

Yes ____ No ____ Why? _____

_____

_____

7. Is it appropriate to wear a turtleneck sweater with a wool tweed knee-length skirt, shoes that blend with the skirt color, sheer hose and a gold pin with discreet earrings for the first meeting with a prospect who is coming to visit the facilities before booking an event with your company?

Yes ____ No ____ Why? _____

_____

_____

THE POWER OF APPROPRIATENESS

As we said earlier, today's professional woman does not need to copy the male "uniform" any longer. You can convey credibility, professionalism and authority while expressing your individuality and complementing your personal characteristics. The new working wardrobe rules are: Wear what is appropriate, comfortable and flattering. Of the three rules, though, *numero uno* is wear what is appropriate— first for your position, second for your figure, third for the season of the year and fourth for the career fashion of the moment. During our seminars with Fortune 500 companies, we invite the participants to discuss a set of posters with photos of professional women wearing different outfits. They select one of the following statements for the outfit that they believe creates that specific type of reaction and/or perception:

a. *Client relates to a competent business look. Reinforces confidence in doing business with company.*

b. *Client senses a "sporty" loose feeling about the company. Lack of seriousness to handle his/her business.*

c. *Client may interpret this as a social occasion, not a business opportunity.*

d. *An outdated look may reflect lack of innovation in the marketplace.*

The following descriptions of outfits are examples of some of the photos that our participants have analyzed. Take a few moments and read each description and choose one of the above statements that you think will describe a client's perception. Circle one of the letters for each outfit. You can select a statement more than once; example, you may decide that there are two descriptions that will create statement c, and so on.

1. Gray-and-white double-breasted houndstooth wool jacket, white silk jewel neck blouse and a black wool skirt.
    a b c d

2. Blue low-cut knit sweater with a short black leather skirt, opaque hose and flat shoes.
    a b c d

3. Brown men's-style plaid suit, long full skirt with a white pleated cotton blouse with a bow tie.
    a b c d

4. Red gabardine coat dress with shawl lapels and gold buttons.
    a b c d

5. A pink, white and blue floral print dress with lace collar and cuffs, high heels and dangling pearl earrings.
    a b c d

This exercise describes your perception of the symbols of a woman's business wardrobe. In the back of the book you will find the perceptions shared by our seminar participants around the country.

Judgments are often formed about a woman on the basis of her attire; thus, on the following pages you will find information on professional dress that will guide you in creating a business look

Matching suit

Unmatched suit

Coat dress

that sends clear messages of capability, professionalism and credibility, and will help you be accepted for your credentials instead of your looks.

BUSINESS LOOK—OPTIONS

When selecting outfits for the office, safe is better than sorry. There are several options for outfits that are internationally accepted as professional looks for women: a suit matched or contrasting; a dress; and a dress with a jacket. Other outfits such as pants or skirts and blouses are not always recognized as professional attire. Therefore, select outfits from a variety of suits, dresses and coordinated separates that are well-made, fit you properly, complement you and are totally professional.

These are the levels of dressiness for the different clothing options for a professional look:

matching suit in a solid color	–most dressy
matching suit in a subtle pattern	–more dressy
unmatched suit	–dressy
dress with a jacket	–dressy
coat dress	–dressy
pant suit (if accepted by organization)	–dressy
dress solid color	–less dressy
dress in small to medium print	–less dressy
skirt and blouse or sweater	–informal
pants and blouse (if accepted by organization)	–casual
shorts and jacket (if accepted by organization)	–casual

THE CREDIBLE BUSINESS SUIT

A suit is the smartest choice for a professional woman today and is the most important item in her wardrobe. Unlike a few years ago, today you don't have to intimidate anyone with huge shoulders. Shoulders are generally softer because of the fashion trend. Suits are more authoritative, though, if they are in dark or rich colors such as navy, black, camel, teal, brown, purple, gray or olive green. Be sure to select a shade that complements your coloring. If you are a very light, fair-skinned person, you will look overpowered by a black or dark suit. Instead, look for shades of teal, blue or blue-gray. If black is your choice or is required by your company, soften it at your neckline with a light top and/or a light color accessory. A patterned suit is another choice; look for tweeds, checks, herringbone and subtle plaids. A red suit is considered a new neutral; red is also a color that tells others you are prepared to stand out and be noticed. Wear it when you are dealing with a large group or convention and you want the participants to listen to what you have to say.

The new suit also has a softer silhouette and simple design. You have many choices: the lapeled jacket either notched or shawl-collared; the V-necked tailored; the box jacket; and the cardigan with soft shoulders. The so-called two-piece or Chanel-style suit, to be worn without a blouse, is another option; even though it is an elegant choice, it is not as versatile to mix and match with other pieces in your wardrobe. You may only be able to match the skirt with other jackets. The non-lapeled and V-necked suit are styles that will accommodate many different necklines. A jacket without lapels would set off blouses with high collars, jewel collars and even a simple V-neckline, allowing you to wear a scarf for variety.

The best fabrics for suits are the all-seasonal fabrics such as gabardine, lightweight wool, wool crepe, silk, linen and rayon blends. Linen is a cool fabric during the warm months, but it wrinkles so much that you will lose your polished look after sitting for more than an hour. Instead, buy linen and silk blends or linen and wool blends which give you comfort without the wrinkles.

When selecting a jacket, pay attention to the details of construction. It is important that you check the quality of a suit because, in general, accepted industry standards are lower for women's clothing than for men's clothing. Look for even trims and hemlines. Your jacket is the most important item in your wardrobe, so select the best quality you can afford.

When selecting a jacket, be sure that it fits you properly. Examine the shoulders: Do they look natural and not severe? Excessive padding at the shoulders is passé. If you want to balance wide hips, try some moderate shoulder pads. Many women wear

Dress with a jacket

Two-piece suit

Three-piece suit

their jackets too small. Your jacket should not wrinkle across the back or under the collar and you must be able to button it easily. Even if you do not button your jacket, it must have enough space for a blouse, vest or sweater; buttons should never tug or pull, be loose or hang. Because you will need to button your jacket before any presentation, be sure that the lapels, buttons and vents look smooth and comfortable when buttoned-up. Check sleeve buttons occasionally for replacement. Be careful not to stretch the pockets from carrying heavy contents. Be sure that the sleeve of the jacket touches your wrist bone; many times a half-inch makes a big difference. If you need the sleeves altered, it is a very worthwhile investment for a polished look. The length of the jacket will depend on two criteria: your body proportions and the fashion trends. You need to choose current styles that flatter your figure and body proportions.

KEEP YOUR JACKET ON!

In our seminars when we discuss the role of a jacket in a professional wardrobe, we invite a participant who is wearing a suit-jacket and a blouse to come to the front of the room. We ask the group to look at her and say out loud what clothing message she is sending. Participants say things like *professional, credible, powerful.* Then we ask her to remove her jacket. The first thing that happens is that she says she feels different, using words like *cold, naked and uncomfortable.* The group says that without the jacket our participant looks *more casual, less credible, less professional.* We call this exercise *"the magic of the jacket."* A jacket is a symbol that imbues the wearer with a feeling of self-confidence and sends out messages of credibility to observers. The jacket is the female equivalent of the male suit and, therefore, it should become the backbone of your wardrobe. Studies on business dress show that in a meeting if a man takes off his jacket and the woman keeps hers on, she has a slight authoritative edge. But if a woman takes off her jacket and the man leaves his on, her position of authority is diminished, even to the point that she may not be perceived as a manager but as support staff.

There are six occasions in which a professional woman benefits from wearing a jacket:

1. When **meeting a client for the first time**. In hospitality, as well as in other industries, first impressions count. The jacket will send a clear message of professionalism. A jacket is an international symbol that means business. If during the first meeting, your client is not wearing a jacket or removes it during the meeting, you may also take off your jacket to make them feel more at ease.

A jacket sends messages of credibility, authority and professionalism.

2. When **giving a presentation**. In this situation a jacket says *"credibility"* and your audience—no matter if they are men or women— tends to pay more attention to a speaker wearing a jacket. You will not see a man giving an important business presentation without his jacket.

3. When **attending meetings**, especially ones in which you know men will participate. It is a matter of space. When attending a meeting, shoulders from suits take up space, so you don't want to diminish your personal power by not wearing a jacket if everyone else is.

4. When **being interviewed**. Whether it is a job interview, a press interview or an internal office interview, your jacket will give you a sense of confidence and credibility.

Absence of jacket diminishes authority.

5. When you work **in an office in which clients or guests drop in** unannounced. If you work in this type of office, your jacket will send a consistent message of professionalism at all times. If your office is not as visible, having a jacket available allows you to be appropriately dressed whenever you learn visitors are stopping by.

6. When you **appear in court**. Chances are that the key players— the judge, attorneys and jurors—will be wearing jackets. They will take you more seriously if your outfit is at the same level of professionalism and your jacket helps you achieve just that. A jacket could be worn over a skirt, over a dress or even over pants or city shorts. A jacket elevates the degree of dressiness and formality of an outfit.

YOUR BLOUSE IS SHOWING

A blouse for a woman is like a tie for a man. It is your signature, the opportunity to express your individuality and to add sparkle to your outfit. Remember that eye contact centers on the oval made by your face, the lapels of your jacket and the upper part of your blouse. This "frame" must send the right messages of quality, coordination and taste. Blouses give your suits, jackets and skirts a finished look and, like suits, should be made of natural fibers or top quality blends such as silk, crepe, challis, cotton and linen. The new washable fabrics are a good choice since caring for them is easy and economical.

You may choose blouses with handsome detailing to make the basic pieces of your wardrobe look new and updated. Sometimes your blouse can make a conservative suit look fresh and sophisticated. The neck styles that work best with most jackets are the jewel neck and high collars. Always invest in a good quality *white* blouse, but a white that is complementary to your coloring could be an ivory, off-white or pure white. A white blouse combines well with most colors of suits and jackets and gives you the option to use accessories—scarves, necklaces and pendants—to set your outfit apart. Sweaters and knits add another dimension to your jackets. Select a turtleneck, a cowl neck or a jewel neck that complements your face shape and neck length. Wearing a knit top with a suit makes the outfit less formal. When I conduct seminars for resort properties, I wear suits and separates with knit tops to achieve a *professional resort look.* A career camisole is another option, and a silk or satin camisole can take your suit into the evening for a dressy occasion. Remember that in this case, you will not want to remove your jacket.

When selecting the right neckline remember that *"the less flesh shown, the more powerful you look."* Two inches above cleavage is considered a conservative neckline. This rule applies to blouses as well as dresses. In addition, with the new policies on sexual harassment, you want to be sure that your clothes elicit only thoughts of respect and professionalism.

You want attention focused on your face not on your chest, so wear appropriate undergarments or a slip-camisole when wearing light-colored blouses. Make sure the blouse is properly fitted with at least one inch of fabric on each side of the bustline, so it looks loose and comfortable. Buttons must remain closed without pulling. When trying on a blouse, do all the arm movements that you usually use on the job, so that you know that the blouse is comfortable.

Here's a tip I learned from my mother who is an accomplished seamstress. When fitting a blouse or dress on me, she would ask me to take my right hand, bend my thumb and put the four fingers together; then I placed the hand in between my underwear and the garment she was fitting. If there was enough space for my hand, the fit was right; if not, the blouse or dress had to be altered. I still use this "home measurement" when I try on ready-made clothes. If your blouse has long sleeves, they should reach to the wrist bone and stick out from the jacket between one-eighth and one-fourth inches. Your blouse should also be longer than your hip bone so you can tuck it in between your underwear and your pantyhose, which helps keep it secure and neat.

Coat dress

DRESSING THE BUSINESS DRESS

In the last few years, the dress has become a welcomed alternative for professional women. After the male uniform look was over, the coat dress was the most popular option for female executives in the '80s; this dress provided a safe transition via its sleek tailoring and notched lapels. Today, you can create a completely professional look with a dress. Designers and manufacturers have created dresses that are authoritative, stylish, comfortable and appropriate for the office. Many dresses today can enhance your image as well as a suit can.

The most important elements when selecting your dresses are quality of construction, color, fabric and design. Look for clean lines and few details. A coat dress made of gabardine is a good first choice. The look should be classic with an impeccable cut. The two-piece dress is also appropriate and a good wardrobe investment since you can mix and match the pieces. Select fabrics such as challis, silk, rayon or a silk blend; these lightweight fabrics team up well with a jacket which can give the two-piece dress a more formal look.

Long sleeve dress

Short-sleeve dress

Shirt dress

AVOID *floral dresses— they are too dressy for the office and send "confusing" messages.*

Solids are easier to accessorize and look dressier. If your prefer prints, be sure the pattern size is small to medium—the size of a quarter or equivalent to a man's tie pattern is appropriate; large patterns are too casual or too dressy for the office. Select patterns such as geometrics, paisleys, stripes, foulards and abstracts. A full floral dress is too dressy for the office and sends confusing messages; colleagues and clients may interpret the situation as a social occasion, not as a business encounter. Florals are symbolic of love, relationships and intimacy; use them in small amounts for blouses and scarves only. Career knits are another option; they are extremely functional and can give you a *suit look.* They are also a woman traveler's best friend.

When purchasing a dress, always replace the self-belt with a fine leather belt in a neutral color that complements the dress; this simple change will elevate the elegance of your dress immediately. As for sleeve length, long-sleeved dresses are more formal and no dress sleeve should be shorter than elbow length, including during warm months. The short-sleeved dress or suit is an especially good choice for a resort property—professional yet informal. Keep a jacket at the office for an instantaneous quick change if you need to raise the level of dressiness during the day or for a go-from-the-office evening event.

TALKING ABOUT SKIRTS

Your skirts are a versatile part of your wardrobe. You can create almost infinite variety by wearing your suit skirts with other jackets, and you can also add other solid or patterned skirts to mix and match with your jackets. By selecting solid skirts in the neutral colors of your palette (page 13 to 17), you will have the flexibility to create combinations with all the colors that complement you.

Since the skirt is such an important element of your wardrobe, be certain it fits properly. A good fit means the waistband is loose enough to insert two fingers allowing it to turn easily; it does not crease or pull across the break of the leg and it hangs from the buttocks in a straight line and does not curve under. If you wear pleats, they should lay flat and not pull open. If the skirt has pockets, they must remain closed. Any tightness in your skirt spoils the total look and sends a careless message; it also draws people's attention to your waist or thighs, which is not where you want it in a business situation.

Then comes the critical question of how short is "too short" for business? Most fashion magazines proclaim that the emphasis for working women is not on power shoulders but legs. This is a risky approach. Fortunately, women no longer allow themselves to be dictated to by the fashion industry about how long or short they should wear their skirts. Even the designers themselves have stated that fashion is no longer a matter of hemlines. This freedom allows women to select a hemline that is comfortable and flattering for them. Today almost any length is fashionable, and short skirts do have a place at the office...with some limitations. When the issue of wearing mini-skirts is discussed in our hospitality seminars, I share how the women who wear them are viewed and reviewed by their managers—male and female: "Your outfit is nice and you are going to make a few people happy today. But at the same time, your outfit could set the stage for sexual harassment." In addition, a mini-skirt can be distracting and they are not user-friendly; it is very difficult to sit comfortably at a desk and it is almost impossible to bend over under any circumstances.

When selecting a short skirt, remember that when you sit down your skirt shortens three inches. Therefore, a skirt that stops around the knee is appropriate for the office. To pinpoint the exact length on you that is both flattering as well as professional, stand up and make a circle with your two thumbs and index fingers and locate it around your kneecap. Any length at the circle, inside the circle or lower than the circle is appropriate. A hemline that is higher than the circle is probably too short and will draw people's attention to your legs instead of to your face where powerful eye contact occurs. When wearing short skirts, combining them with matching stockings in semi-opaque styles gives you a more professional look; sheer skin-colored and patterned hose draw undue attention to the legs.

If your legs are not an asset and short skirts do not appeal to you, you can minimize attention there by wearing longer, flowing hemlines with matching hosiery. Taller women look great in longer lengths if the skirts are not too bulky. Very full, long swirling skirts are too social or casual for the office. If you like this style, try one cut on the bias which will give you the movement without excess volume. Long pleated or semi-pleated skirts are a better option. When selecting a long, narrow skirt, walk around the store and experience how comfortable it is. One of the latest trends is a long skirt with a slit. The height of the slit should be measured the same as you do the short skirt since once you sit down, that is how high your skirt will open.

PANTS OR NO PANTS?

"In 1990, I gave my first speech to Congress and received hundreds of calls. I thought the response was to my speech, but I had unknowingly become the first woman to wear pants on the House floor," said Congresswoman Susan Molinari. When will pants cease to be grounds for debate? Many companies actively discourage or specifically prohibit women from wearing trousers while others accept them under certain conditions. In 1989 when I was planning a seminar for a hotel in Washington, D.C., the general manager told me that the female executives were allowed to wear pant suits, and that this new policy was giving his hotel an international edge. It did not surprise me since Scandinavian and German women have a good laugh over the U.S. debate about wearing pants in the office; trousers are widely worn by working women in these countries. At the same time, pants are not yet interpreted internationally as a symbol of a female professional as much as a skirted suit is.

The acceptance of pants as an option for women in hospitality is changing slowly but surely. If wearing pants is not accepted in your company yet, remember that controversial clothing can get you the wrong kind of attention. And, unfortunately, some women have abused a pants-allowed policy by wearing poor quality trousers or stirrup pants with a blouse or sweater. This is one of the reasons why some companies do not want to open the door to include pants as an accepted option since they fear that some women will cross that fine line between comfort and unprofessional attire.

If pants are accepted in your company, always wear a jacket.

Pants without a jacket lack professionalism and credibility.

If pants are an accepted option for business attire in your organization, matched and unmatched pant suits are the styles that will express your professionalism and credibility. Matching trousers and jacket is the more formal option; trousers with an unmatched jacket is less dressy. The best pant suit options are those in elegant neutral colors in good quality fabrics. The more substantial the weight and texture of the fabric the better. Choose gabardine, wool flannel, wool crepe, tweeds and herringbones. Select patterns that look like *solids* from a distance. Always complement a pant suit with a leather belt and appropriate shoes. A medium heel pants shoe makes the pant suit formal and elegant. A lower heel makes it less dressy. When wearing trousers, always wear earrings and other accessories such as pins, scarves or necklaces. Also remember that when wearing pants you will be noticed more, which demands a high quality trouser as well as impeccable cut and fit. Follow the same guidelines as for the skirt: Pleats must remain closed without pulling, pockets need to remain closed and the waistband should be loose enough to insert two fingers. Adjust the trousers' hem to mid-heel length for an elegant polished look. Avoid too short a hem when you wear trousers.

Accessories complement an unmatched pantsuit for a professional look.

PUTTING THEM ALL TOGETHER

When combining articles of clothing, you may be able to mix and match to achieve different looks depending on the occasion, or depending on the type of property you work in. In a city hotel, your look may need to be more *corporate* to appeal to your guests and clients. At a resort, you may need to have a less formal but still professional look. In both cases, in the hospitality industry there are times and situations in which women are expected to wear more casual attire, such as for a barbecue, a patio party or just an outdoor function at which a tailored wool suit would not be appropriate, since clients and guests will be in their khakis and polo shirts, pants and blouses.

So, let's look at the different fabrics that make a more *corporate-dressy* look versus a resort-casual look:

Pair pants with a sweater and a jacket for a less dressy professional look.

DRESSY— *solids or small prints in fine weaves*
worsted wool
wool crepe gabardine
gabardine
crepe
crepe de Chine
satin (evening wear)
cashmere (evening wear)
charmuse (evening wear)
jacquard
tissue faile

LESS DRESSY— *solids or medium prints in medium weaves*
herringbone
challis
jersey
knit
broadcloth
oxford cloth
cotton pique
raw silk
tweed - patterned
linen
linen/blends
handkerchief-weight linen
wool flannel
rayon

CASUAL—*solids or medium to large prints in coarser, looser weaves*
corduroy
denim
madras
seersucker
tapestry
poplin

Remember that the finer the weave and the shinier the fabric, the dressier the garment. Matte finish is less dressy. When making combinations, mix: dressy with dressy

dressy with less dressy

less dressy with casual

casual with casual

Do not mix dressy with casual

Avoid leather or suede for garments since these fabrics are considered sensual and, therefore, send mixed messages in office settings; use them for accessories only—belts, shoes and handbags. Forego shiny fabrics for day; wear them for evening or social events only.

THE PROFESSIONAL RESORT LOOK

If your position requires a *professional resort look,* your goal is to select clothes and accessories that will make you look more approachable, friendly and less formal but still professional, without intimidating your casually dressed guest who may be wearing shorts and a T-shirt or resort wear. You can achieve this look by choosing less constructed clothing, separates, sweaters, knit tops in more textured fabrics and by using more color and creating more interesting and creative color combinations.

When we interviewed many resort properties around the country for this book, we found that the clothing options for women managers in resorts is broader than for those in city hotels. Ninety-nine percent of the respondents said that at their properties, besides wearing the traditional suits, dresses and skirts, women wear pants suits. In the resorts located in a warmer climate, pants with no jackets were also appropriate. The walking short—also called the *City Short*—was mentioned by most of the companies as another alternative for the resort look. When selecting this look, which consists of long shorts and a jacket, be sure that the jacket is long enough to give you a suited look. If you choose to wear culottes, remember that they look better teamed up with smart jackets, so they give you a comfortable but still professional look. When selecting culottes, be sure not to have too much volume, and select a good quality fabric.

When choosing fabrics, select from the less dressy or dressy

Less constructed jackets are a smart option for a professional resort look.

A shirt dress for a resort look.

Pants are accepted as a professional look in most resorts.

Textured fabrics are appropriate for resort look.

Long jackets give the "city shorts" a professional resort look.

category (ones with a matte finish) and mix them with fabrics from the less dressy list. Example: A gabardine skirt with a wool flannel jacket and a knit top; or, a linen-blend pant suit with a cotton blouse.

Select *less dressy accessories* such as:
    lower heel shoes
    colored shoes
    matte finish necklaces, earrings, pins
    colorful discreet accessories
    gold, silver, copper buttons
    pocket squares
    scarves
    subtle stones
    ivory
    chains
    chokers
    sashes
    colored leather or patent belts

When completing the outfit described above (gabardine skirt, flannel jacket and knit top), add a challis scarf or an ivory necklace or pin with earrings, a matte-finish leather belt and medium heel shoes for a complete *professional resort look*.

ACCESSORIES

Shoes, belts, jewelry and scarves can take your outfit from ordinary to extraordinary. When you wear your clothes over and over again, changing the accessories will make them look new. "Every season, I recommend that my clients invest the amount equivalent to one complete outfit in accessories," says my colleague Mary Elizabeth Kaiser. This is the least expensive way to stay fashionably up-to-date.

SHOES AND HOSE

Select shoes that are comfortable as well as professional; after all, you will be on your feet most of the time. Some women care more about the color than the quality or their shoes, but it should be just the opposite. Buying good quality shoes is an investment that affects your well-being. If you are uncomfortable throughout the day, this discomfort will keep you from performing your work with energy and enthusiasm. A medium heel pump (one-and-one-half to two inches) is a perfect choice. I call the pump your best accessory friend; it is elegant, simple and can be combined with any outfit. Avoid open toes or sandal styles which are too dressy or too casual for the office. The heel of a shoe can alter the dressiness of your outfit: the higher the heel, the dressier the look; the lower the heel the less dressy. When wearing short, knee-length skirts, a medium to high heel is appropriate. When wearing longer narrow or pleated skirts, select a lower heel. Avoid flats which are too casual for the office.

Replacing the heels or entire soles with quality leather or rubber will ensure longevity. When buying suede, treat them with water-resistant spray before wearing. Store your shoes in a cupboard or closet between wearings using wooden shoe trees to help keep their shape. Resting shoes for two or three days before wearing them again will allow the leather to recuperate and will help your shoes last longer. Your feet will also appreciate wearing a different shoe each day, so they can also recuperate from the sensitive spots that got rubbed during the wearing. And, of course, not only men have to keep their shoes shined regularly. One of the pleasures of traveling for me is getting my shoes shined and reading the newspaper while waiting for my plane. So whether at the airport or at home, giving your shoes a regular shine will give you a polished, professional look.

Select hose in your nude shade, sheer or semi-opaque. Avoid patterned hose and colored hose such as red, burgundy, purple, green and pink. Also, do not try to create the impression of having a tan by wearing "suntan" hosiery. It does not work and makes you look *inexpensive*.

To confirm this approach of not bringing *colored attention* to your legs, let me share the result of a poll conducted with professional men and women in 1989. The male professionals listed three things about their female colleagues that they considered unprofessional:

- chipped nail polish
- heavy fragrance
- colored hose.

If you want to know what the women said about their male colleagues, turn to page 51.

SHOES, HOSE AND HEMLINES— THE RIGHT COMBINATION

While men struggle with choosing the right tie, shirt and suit combinations, women have difficulties selecting the right hose and shoes for a hemline. This is one of the most common questions that we get in our seminars. The main idea is that you do not want to draw attention to your legs in a business encounter. You want your outfit to begin in a flow of color from the bottom going up without breaking the continuity at the leg area. You do not want anything in your outfit that makes a *visual or mental noise*. Light hose in the middle of a dark hemline and dark shoes will make a *visual noise* by bringing attention to it. Follow the *Golden Rule* for combining shoes, hose and hemlines:

Hose must be your nude shade, same shade as shoes or lighter, *never darker*.

The following chart will help you select the right shoes and hose for your hemlines. Look at the outfit you want to combine in the column that says Hemlines. Look for the shoes and hose options on the same line.

Do: Select hose in your nude, same shade as shoes or lighter.

Avoid: Hose darker than shoes make a "visual noise" that attracts attention to legs.

HEMLINES	HOSE	SHOES
Ivory or light color	ivory, cream	ivory, cream
Taupe	taupe, light gray, beige	taupe, gray, beige
Camel/golden brown	beige or golden tone	camel, brown, black
Brown	sheer brown	brown
Gray	gray, medium taupe or gray or sheer black	gray, black

Navy	sheer navy, gray, or sheer black	navy, black
Black	sheer black, gray or almost black	black
Bright colors: red, blue, royal, coral	ivory cream taupe gray sheer black beige	ivory bone taupe gray black camel, golden brown
Dark colors: purple, rust, burgundy, dark green, teal	sheer navy sheer back gray sheer brown	navy black gray olive or brown
Prints in medium tones	Select a neutral background color and choose the appropriate hose and shoes. Example: For a gray and yellow print, follow instructions for gray.	

OTHER ACCESSORIES

When selecting accessories, look for simple, classic styles in medium to large sizes. Well-designed "significant" jewelry will create a look that is individual and distinctive. Invest in a good quality watch and avoid plastic, sport, calculators or alarm watches. Avoid dangling or too large earrings. Dangling earrings or anything that moves or makes noise creates a *visual or mental noise* which detracts from the eye contact. When wearing strands of pearls, stones or chains, limit the strands to three. More than three becomes too dressy for a business look. One ring per hand is enough for a polished look. Keep bracelets to a minimum. Any bracelets that move or make noise will work against your professional look. Try a single bracelet or a few fine ones together with your watch for interest.

Avoid wearing too many pieces. How many are *too many?* After you have put on the last accessory and think you are ready, look in a mirror and count points. The 15-point check-up before leaving for work will alert you if you have gone too far. Count each shoe, your stockings, your jacket and blouse and your skirt, if it is differ-

ent from the jacket. Bright colors count two points and bright nail polish and red hair each count one point. Count all accessories including bracelets, necklaces, each earring, brooches and scarves. If the number exceeds 15, you've overdone it. Also, any time you are not sure about wearing a particular accessory, the answer is probably *NO!*, so leave it off.

MAKING UP FOR BUSINESS

Studies conducted in America and Europe confirm that women who wear makeup earn more money and advance faster than their colleagues who don't. In the mid-1980s, one corporation funded a study to find out the effect that makeup and grooming had on women at work. Photographs and resumes were sent out to top personnel officers; in some of the photos women wore makeup and in some they did not. The officers were asked which of the women they would hire and how much would they pay, assuming the need for a professional with their qualifications. The results showed that not only were the candidates wearing makeup more likely to be offered jobs, but they were offered salaries between 20 and 25 percent higher than the un-made-up women.

Makeup for professional women is as important as their outfit. The good news is that an appropriate makeup is one that is well blended and looks minimal. Women who wear too much makeup or too garish colors are considered to have as poor an image—or worse—than women who wear none. A natural, blended makeup is one that gives you a fresh look without calling undue attention to it. If you do not like to wear makeup or have never worn it, begin with blush and lipstick. A lipstick affects the look of your eyes. Look at yourself before you apply lipstick and pay attention to your eyes. It is vital that you select a lipstick that is in harmony with your coloring (see list below). Now, apply your flattering lipstick and focus on your eyes again and see the effect it has on them; they will look brighter and sparkling.

Wearing blush and lipstick are essential to achieving a business makeup look. Therefore, be sure that the colors you choose complement your coloring. Have you ever seen a person with golden skin, golden green eyes and medium brown hair with gold high-

lights wearing fuchsia lipstick? When you look at her all you focus on is the lipstick which, even if her clothes are professional and exquisitely put together, breaks the harmony of the total look. When choosing your makeup, follow your natural coloring and select from the colors listed below. Some common sense applies when choosing shades for a particular outfit. For example, when wearing red, wear the version of red that complements you, either a true, blue red (cool), or a yellow red (warm). If you are in the Deep category, wear red lipstick when you wear red, black or green. If your outfit has olive green, maroon, brown, peach, coral or any golden tones, avoid lipsticks in pink, rose or fuchsia, even if you do look good in those shades.

LIPSTICKS AND BLUSH SHADES

DEEP	LIGHT	WARM	COOL	BRIGHT	SUBTLE
true red	pinks	corals	pinks	clear pinks	corals
burgundy	corals	warm reds	burgundy	true reds	rose
	coral red	rust	cool red	clear corals	soft reds
		honey			honey
					mahogany

rust *
fuchsia **
* Wear if you have warm undertones (golden skin tone, warm toned eyes and warm tones in you hair—confirm with an Image Consultant).
** Wear if you have cool undertones (rose brown, olive skin, brown or black eyes and you look sallow in golden tones—confirm with an Image Consultant).

MAKEUP TIPS

- Use the proper tools to apply your makeup; good quality brushes make your job easier.
- Loose powder or foundation is essential. Select a foundation that matches the color of your skintone at the jawline. Use powder to set liquid foundation for a natural look.
- Blush should give you a healthy glow and not appear as cheek flames or cheek balls. Apply a small amount with a blush brush, stroking along your cheeks at an angle toward your temple. If you need more color, apply a bit more blush and repeat. Finish with translucent powder.

- An eye shadow base smoothed over the lid before applying eye shadow, helps your eye shadow last ten to 12 hours without creasing.
- To keep eyebrows looking neat, apply some clear mascara or hair gel to a spare, clean lash wand and brush eyebrows up and into place.
- Lipstick will stay for hours with this technique: first, apply foundation to the lips; then line lips with lip pencil in the same shade or lighter than your lipstick shade; next fill in the entire lip area with the lip pencil; then apply lipstick—ideally with a lip brush—taking care to stay between the lines.
- Touch up your powder and lipstick a couple of times during the day.

Your Hair

Your hair is considered your most visible accessory. It wraps your face and can complement or destroy the polished look you have carefully put together. One company hired me to coach a very effective female manager who was sabotaging her career by not controlling her long fuzzy hair. It was the focus of attention and the subject of conversation after every important meeting. We suggested she visit a hair "designer" who could give her a stylish cut for her hair type, and then to show the cut the same day to her regular hair dresser so he or she could inexpensively keep up the new style. If your hair is hard to manage, a shorter haircut could be a solution. If your hair is longer than your shoulders, you will want to pull it back in a neat style—either bowed or French-twisted—so your face is visible and your hair is not a distraction.

If you color your hair, bring out the natural tones or bring back the highlights that you once had. Any color you select should make you look natural and healthy. When contemplating a new color, it is best to seek professional advice; a colorist will help you select the most natural and complementary color for you. Be sure that the new color blends with your eyebrows and does not make such a statement that everyone will notice your hair first.

FINISHING TOUCHES FOR YOUR FACE

Besides the correct makeup, you want to select a flattering hair style and accessories that complement your face. Following are suggestions for hair styles and earrings for each of the seven face shapes. These suggestions may differ from the ones given in fashion and beauty books and articles. My approach to achieving balance and harmony for our personal or professional look is to follow and echo the lines of our bodies and face shapes, instead of trying to change them. I believe that the face shape you were born with is perfect for you. Trying to achieve the so-called ideal oval face is a waste of time and effort. I tried for years and it just did not work. I have very obvious facial angles. When I put on round earrings and accessories and got a curved hairstyle in an attempt to hide my angular face and make it appear rounder, I looked ridiculous. I invite you to identify your face shape with the description below, asking someone else to confirm your determination.

Then accept it and celebrate it!

Donna Fujii in the book *Color With Style* gives the following guidelines:

Oval

If your face is oval, the length is longer than the width. Your face is not too long or too wide.

Hairstyle: You can wear most hairstyles. Symmetrical lines work well with your balanced features. Let it flow free with soft waves around your face or pull it back to show off your features.

Earrings: Most shapes work well. Avoid extremely long shapes that can elongate your face.

OVAL

Oblong

The length of your face is noticeably longer than the width. Brow bone, cheekbones and jawline are almost the same width.

Hairstyle: Wear bangs and a mid-length style with some fullness at the sides. Avoid long, straight hair, height on top, an exposed hairline or hair pulled back.

Earrings: Wide, curved shapes will create width through the middle of your face. Avoid long, narrow or dangling earrings as this will elongate your face.

OBLONG

Square

The brow bone, cheekbone, and jawline are approximately the same width. The length of the face is short in proportion to the width.

Hairstyle: Add height to the crown, using layered or asymmetrical cuts. Swirly and light waves at the temples and jawline will soften the bone structure. Keep your cut in a medium to short length if your neck is short. Avoid solid straight bangs.

Earrings: Medium size, angular with soft corners work well. Avoid squares, round and too big earrings.

SQUARE

Diamond

Cheekbones are wider than brow bone and jawline. The jawline is angular and pointed.

Hairstyle: To balance cheekbones, add fullness at the top of the head and below the ear. Bangs will add fullness to the forehead. Avoid exposing hairline and ears. Avoid a haircut that is too long as it will elongate your face.

Earrings: Wear earrings with angles close to your face. Squares and triangles will work well. Avoid curved, long or dangling earrings.

DIAMOND

Triangle

Jawline is significantly wider than brow bone and cheekbone.

Hairstyle: Keep hairline away from jawline. Either short or neck-long hair works well. Look for fullness.

Earrings: Choose earrings that do not hit the jawline. Angular shapes that sweep upward are a good choice. Avoid curved shapes.

TRIANGLE

Heart

The forehead and cheekbones are wider than the jawline, creating a prominent V shaped chin.

Hairstyle: Bangs will break the forehead width. Avoid a top-heavy look and extremely short hair styles. Keep your hair chin- to shoulder-length.

Earrings: Select oval shapes that are broader at the bottom; this will add width near the chin line.

HEART

ROUND

Round

Cheekbones are wider than the brow bone and jaw line. Outline is curved in a circular shape.

Hairstyle: Build hair up on top of the head. Keep it in a medium to short length if your neck is also short. An off-center left or right part above your eye breaks up the face. Avoid very short styles or a center part.

Earrings: Choose earrings with curved lines that are longer than they are wide. Avoid too big or round earrings. Longer or dangling earrings that are not too narrow will also work well.

FINAL TIPS

- Wearing glasses makes you look older and more credible.
- Wear clear not tinted glasses for easier communication.
- Clear nail polish is the best. Colored nail polish should complement lipstick color.
- Avoid any garment that is too low, too tight or too clingy.
- Use a fountain pen.
- Use a leather attaché case in one of the neutrals of your wardrobe.
- It is acceptable to carry an attaché case plus a small handbag.
- Choose accessories that do not need constant attention. If you have to worry about something slipping, take it off.
- Your fragrance *should not enter the room before you do and should not stay a week later.* Less is more!
- Invest in a full-length mirror; it will become a truthful best friend.

A Quick Check
Before Facing the World

Before you leave for work or a social engagement, examine with your best friend—a full-length mirror—the overall picture you present and the details from head to toe. Make the necessary changes, add or remove accessories and be sure your appearance and grooming are impeccable. This daily exercise will take just a few minutes but the confidence of being well dressed will be worth it. If you can check all the points, you are ready to face the world!

Jacket
- Does not wrinkle across the back or under the collar
- Buttons easily
- Sleeves at wrist bone
- Does not pull across the back
- Pockets remain closed; any pleat or dart must lie flat

Blouse
- Long sleeve should be at wrist bone
- Buttons must remain closed with at least one inch of fabric on each side of the bust line
- Longer than the hip bone
- Avoid sleeveless blouses

Skirt
- Pleats should not pull open
- No crease or pull across break of leg
- Skirt should easily turn around your body
- Straight skirts should hang from buttocks in a straight line and not curve under
- Not shorter than "around the knee"
- Loose enough for two fingers to be inserted in waistband
- No visible lines under skirt

DRESS

- coat dress, shirt dress or two piece
- conservative neckline (2" above cleavage)
- medium to long sleeve
- medium to small print
- avoid floral prints

SLACKS

- Pleats remain closed
- Zippers and closings must lie flat
- Long enough to break in front
- Do not wrinkle across the front
- Fall straight from buttocks
- Waistband loose enough to allow two fingers to be inserted
- Panty line must not show
- Worn with jacket for a professional look

SHOES & HOSE

- Select neutral shades
- No sandals or "strappy" shoes
- Avoid too high or narrow heels
- Avoid flats
- Hose color does not bring attention to leg area
- Choose natural color hose that blend with hemline
- Hose color is nude, same shade as shoes or lighter, never darker
- No colored hose (red, purple, pink)
- Avoid patterned or textured hose

JEWELRY

- Small to medium earrings, simple styles
- Avoid dangling or large hooped earrings
- Avoid noisy jewelry or pieces that move
- Avoid too many pieces
- No tinted glasses

MAKEUP AND GROOMING

- Wear blended, natural makeup
- Choose simple, carefree hair styles
- For colored hair, avoid roots showing
- Avoid extreme fashion styles and colors
- If your hair falls below the shoulders, pull it back
- Keep fingernails short to medium length
- Avoid too bright colors (fuchsia-orange-purple) in nail polish
- No chipped nails
- Avoid dark lingerie with light clothing
- No slip showing below hemline
- Avoid high split in skirt
- No slip showing between split in skirt
- Avoid heavy fragrance

Casual Days in Hospitality?

$\mathcal{T}$he trend of casual dressing in American corporations has been spreading rapidly in the past few years. Business clothing began relaxing in the '70s on the west coast, and in the late '80s this trend began to spread around the country. In a 1992 study, Levi Straus & Company found that 67 percent of 500 companies surveyed allow casual dress days all or part of the time. Some companies have established "dress-down" Fridays, allowing workers to dress casually. Companies intend that casual days will loosen the sense of formality in corporate hallways, encouraging workers at all levels to communicate better with each other. Some companies say that it leads to better morale and saves people money on their wardrobe.

However, when employees and corporations across the country evaluate the impact of casual days there are conflicting reports:

Some companies have found that this has been an easy way to boost morale and it has served as an office "equalizer," making it easy for people to talk to each other. Some report that going casual helps employees relax and builds team spirit because everyone is dressed similarly. Some say that their employees would like casual days to be allowed year-round and not only on certain days. "I can work better because I am more comfortable moving around," says one female employee. In creative fields such as advertising, fashion and entertainment, as well as in creative positions in high-tech companies, it seems that dressing down is appropriate and conducive to creativity and innovation.

The added value of casual days as a wardrobe saver has not been equally true for both genders. While some men can save money with polo shirts and khaki pants, women complain that now they need not only a business wardrobe but a casual one as well. This confirms the theory that "women shop to look attractive and unique, men shop to look like the other guys," and in achieving these goals, it seems the first group needs to spend more money!

Some men, though, are also put off by the idea of wearing a polo shirt to work. They prefer to keep the confident feeling that comes when they "suit up." In a late fall 1994 article in *USA Today,* David Wolfe, a fashion forecaster, said that the "Casual Friday" movement was mostly a Madison Avenue marketing ploy to make men buy something, *anything.* "And it worked," he said. Men bought a lot of casual wear. For a while. Now major designers admit that many customers never really wanted to toss their suits. "Wearing casual buisness clothing in a troubled economy is misguided," says Richard Martin of the Metropolitan Museum of Art's Costume Institute.

While some companies brag about the positive results of dress-down days, others have found that as they have relaxed their dress code, the performance has relaxed as well. In some places this low productivity began to change when, instead of an occasional day in which people dressed casually, it was institutionalized on certain days during the week or month. Once it became the norm, people did not pay as much attention to the issue and they went back to business as usual.

Some corporate executives tell us that they regret the dress-down policy. "Casual Fridays" have become "Friendly Fridays," they say. Men still look similar when they dress casual. Khakis and polo shirts still give men a sense of uniformity. When women get casual, they have more options in interpreting what casual means: tight stirrup pants with a revealing top is often what some women consider casual. With this kind of attire, instead of being looked at as an efficient team member, women are looked at as attractive females, becoming more vulnerable to sexual harassment.

Other corporations are not allowing dress-down days. One of our corporate clients says, "It is about credibility. We deal with international clients, and it would be an insult to our foreign clients to conduct a business meeting in casual attire." Some financial institutions do not have causal days, either. "We feel that our customers expect us to dress professionally because we handle their money," says a spokesperson for a bank.

During the summer of '94 while working on this book, we conducted a survey around the country to find out whether casual days are practiced in the hospitality industry. We found that none of the companies we interviewed have established casual days at the *property level*. "Hospitality is a seven-days-a-week business," said one of the respondents. "A client would feel offended if, at their wedding reception, a manager, who was assisting with the most important event of their lives, was wearing casual wear; it would damage the company's credibility. We don't have the same luxury that other industries have today to relax our dress standards."

However, we found that several of the major, large hospitality organizations have dress-down days at their *corporate offices only*. Some of them do not call them "casual days," they call them "relaxed business attire days." Some of them were experimenting with the policy for the first time during the summer of 1994, and did not know if they would continue in the future.

As for guidelines, we found everything from none to loose to very specific. One respondent defined their company policy as: "Use common sense and when in doubt ask." One of the large hotel companies asked us to conduct seminars to assist employees at their corporate offices in achieving a casual look that is still professional. This is now a common request, since companies as well as employees are having difficulties in knowing where to draw the clothing line between relaxed and sloppy attire.

What one company considers appropriate for casual days, others may not accept. Jeans, sneakers and T-shirts are accepted in some companies, while other places allow only khakis and polo shirts for men. Others require that men's shirts have collars and that women wear blouses with pants. Other places ask women to wear jackets if they choose to wear city shorts, and sleeveless dresses or halter tops were universally disallowed. It is frequent that even within the same company, the policy varies, depending on the departments. Many departments serve different customers, either internal or external. Some companies, when they have meetings with clients on Fridays, will let the clients know that it is a casual dress day and that they are welcome to dress casually, also.

As we can see, the full effect of this trend for business casual dress has not been measured across corporate America as yet. In fact, this trend is just beginning to take place in hospitality at the headquarters level. Dress is such a vital element of your professional presence that losing what can be a powerful visual tool may be to your disadvantage. Unfortunately, this affects women more than it affects men. Casual does not mean sloppy. It means comfortable, appropriate and attractive. It is a matter of balance and good sense. Our advice is that, when you need to dress down for work, dress casually but professionally. Dressing conservatively is a safe strategy. Before you leave home, it would be smart to look in a full-length mirror and ask yourself: "If I run into anyone from within or outside the company, would I need to apologize or explain my outfit?" If your answer is "yes", I suggest you go back and make some changes.

Susan Bixler, a nationally known image consultant, says: *"If you want the job, look the part; if you want the promotion, look promotable; if you want respect, dress as well or better than your industry standards."* Robert Pante, also a well-recognized image expert, recommends to professionals: *"Dress for the job you want, not for the one you have; you are already there."* Use your professional appearance including grooming, clothes and accessories to your advantage. When trading for comfort, avoid any risk that may affect your credibility and professionalism. The price may be too high.

UNIVERSAL
STANDARDS

*M*ost of us have probably had the experience of sitting or standing next to someone in public—say on a bus or in line at the theater—and being assailed by an unpleasant body odor. We ask (only to ourselves, of course) how could anyone leave their home without even minimal bathing? But the fact is that people do leave their homes for work and social engagements without performing basic grooming. It's also a fact that various cultures have differing standards concerning what constitutes basic grooming.

For example, soon after marrying my husband from Ohio, my in-laws came to visit us in Washington, D.C. After welcoming them into our new house, I asked them if they wanted to take a shower. My surprised husband blurted out, "Why? Do you think they are dirty?" After blushing with embarrassment, I understood that this custom from my native Colombia was not a custom here in the states. In Colombia, when your overnight guests arrive, they expect you to offer them a shower so they can freshen up after a usually hot and sweaty trip. In countries at or near the equator, taking a shower is considered a pleasant ritual necessary for comfort. In contrast, there are cultures in which a bath or shower is deemed necessary only weekly or bi-weekly.

So, how do we agree on appropriate hygiene and grooming habits that will ensure that we present an impeccable professional appearance, regardless of our country of origin or whether we are uniformed or non-uniformed employees? The answer is by following the grooming guidelines that have been adapted by most hospitality organizations around the world as a way to provide quality service that is appreciated by all customers and guests—no matter where they are from. I invite you to use the following questionnaire for self-feedback. Let's see how your current grooming practices measure up to these international standards.

Answer the following questions with either "Yes" or "No". Give yourself a point for every "Yes" and add up your score. If you can't answer yes to all the parts of the question, do not give yourself a point. When you find a question that does not apply to you, give yourself a point anyway, if your answer would theoretically be "Yes."

WOMEN'S CHECKLIST

1. Is your hair clean, neat and in a conservative style?
2. If you color your hair, is the color a natural shade without tell-tale roots?
3. If your hair is longer than shoulder-length, is it pulled back neatly?
4. Do you check your shoulders for dandruff and regularly brush it off during the day?
5. Is your makeup well-blended and natural (not too bright or in frosted shades)? Note: If your job requires an elaborate makeup for the nightclub or disco, you may give yourself a point for bright or exaggerated makeup.
6. Are your nails short or medium size (no longer than one-eighth to one-fourth inches at the tip)?
7. Is your nail polish freshly applied and not chipped?
8. Is your nail polish a light color? (Too bright colors would include orange, purple and fuchsia.)
9. If you use cologne or perfume, do you use it sparingly?
10. Do you take a daily shower or bath, use a deodorant, brush and floss your teeth and rinse with mouthwash?

MEN'S CHECKLIST

1. Is your hair clean, short (does not touch your shirt collar) and neatly combed?
2. Are nose and ear hair trimmed?
3. If you have a mustache or beard, are they well-trimmed? (Mustache not touching the upper lip?)
4. Do you check your shoulders for dandruff and regularly brush it off during the day?
5. Are your fingernails short and clean?
6. If you use cologne or after shave lotion, do you use it sparingly?
7. Do you take a daily shower or bath, use a deodorant, brush and floss your teeth and rinse with mouthwash?

How did you score? Women's score ___ Men's Score ___.

If you are female and your score is ten or if you are male and your score is seven, congratulations! You follow the basic grooming elements needed to make an excellent impression each and every day.

If you answered "No" to any of the above questions, you may want to make some changes to ensure that your personal grooming elicits respect from your coworkers and customers.

WHY STANDARDS?

The hospitality industry is a people business. We have daily face-to-face contact with our fellow employees, customers and suppliers. In this communication process, eye contact is one of the most powerful tools we have. For this reason, good grooming becomes an essential way to facilitate good communication. For example, we certainly don't want to be distracted from our duties by an unruly lock of hair falling in our face, and we certainly don't want our customers to be distracted by this either. Good grooming—be it of hair, body or face—keeps the focus where it belongs, on the business at hand.

FROM HEAD...

For women, hair that is worn longer than shoulder length, is styled in an exaggerated fashion or is multi-colored usually is a distraction. People will focus on your hair instead of what you are saying.

For men, beards and mustaches are tending to disappear in business in the '90s. A clean face facilitates face-to-face communication with coworkers, customers and suppliers. Mary Spillane, an image consultant from England, writes in her book *Presenting Yourself: A Professional Image Guide for Men*: "Men who are clean-shaven have a better chance of getting a job, and being readily accepted in business." But you can bet that employers will never tell a person that the reason they didn't get hired was because of grooming issues like this one. Beards are used to cover facial imperfections and, if this is why you choose to wear one, it's a good idea to discuss this with the interviewer. You certainly do not need to justify your beard to others, though. You just have to pay extra attention to your grooming and dressing in order to present an impeccable appearance.

TALKING HANDS

In the hospitality field, hands are our main tool of the trade. We serve our customers with both our words and our hands. Cleanliness, then, is a must for male and female employees, regardless of position. Female employees who wear nail polish should keep it freshly applied and chip-free. It is best to choose a light to medium shade that complements the color of your outfit or uniform. For example, if you wear a peach or golden tone uniform, pink nail polish will clash with it. Also, the color of your nail polish should blend with the color of your lipstick. Red lipstick and pink nail polish do not blend and would be distracting to your customer. Clear nail polish is probably the best choice for the professional female, whether she wears a uniform or regular clothes.

THE EFFECTS OF SCENTS

Fragrance can be either an asset or a liability to your profession-al image. After shave lotions, cologne and perfumes must be used sparingly. One president of a large corporation took to climbing 17 flights of stairs to his office every morning. His employees thought this was part of his fitness routine, but they were wrong. As he put it, "I get sick when I get into the elevator at 8 o'clock in the morn-ing with all those heavy fragrances." Many people are allergic to perfumes, so we must be considerate of our coworkers and cus-tomers. Your fragrance should not enter a room before you do, and it should not be there a week later!

Also know that scents can remind us of certain people and evoke emotional responses. One of my colleagues went to a meeting with the president of a company that was considering using her ser-vices as an image consultant. When she shook hands with the potential client, he said: "You smell just like my ex-wife." Probably not the best way to begin a sales meeting! While we may have to risk wearing the "wrong" fragrance, (after all, how could my friend have known that her chosen perfume that day would stir old and presumably unpleasant memories) we can at least use it sparingly.

Also, we must take care not to wear a fragrance that is so attrac-tive to the opposite sex that we're sending the wrong signals to coworkers and clients.

Simple, daily grooming routines provide the perfect founda-tion for our professional appearance and ensure that we proceed with confidence in all our business communications: a daily show-er or bath with soap; a daily application of deodorant (reapply more frequently if your work causes you to sweat profusely); clean hands and tended nails; a light cologne or perfume and good oral hygiene will ensure that our bodies do not interfere with the qual-ity of our service. In addition, a flattering and easy-to-care-for hair style and makeup will frame our faces and enhance essential eye-to-eye contact.

WEARING YOUR UNIFORM WITH CLASS

*W*ell-groomed employees—whether uniformed or not—project a sense of confidence to the publics they serve and, in the hospitality industry, add to the overall credibility of the property they represent. When customers, guests and coworkers meet you for the first time, an impression is formed just like a photograph records a moment frozen in time. It is difficult, if not impossible, to retake the same photo and, so too, it is difficult for people to change their first impression of you. Which is why it is so important that you present a well-groomed appearance—one that says "I can handle the job, I have exactly what you need and you can trust me."

This chapter offers you an opportunity to take an honest look at how you present yourself and see which aspects of your appearance are supporting your image of excellence and which may be letting you down in your career. Many of the issues that we will examine are sensitive; they cover all aspects of good grooming from hygiene to clothing. But in order for me to fulfill my promise to you to cover all elements that contribute to a positive first impression, no issue can be left out. What follows is a complete manual for self-feedback about your professional appearance.

WHY DO WE WEAR UNIFORMS?

Uniforms provide us with a sense of order, reassurance and split-second recognition. Think of a police officer, a nurse or someone in the military. People in uniforms exude authority and inspire confidence before they even have a chance to assist us.

In the hospitality industry, uniformed employees send a clear message to a guest: "I am here to serve you." A uniform alerts people to your particular job responsibility and assures them that you have the expertise to help them. Your uniform also shows that you are part of a TEAM! When the members of a team wear their uniform with pride, it enhances the image that the company wants to convey to its customers. In our Image Impact and Gracious Hospitality seminars, we discuss the bond of trust between you and your company. Specifically, when you are issued a uniform, you have been entrusted to accomplish a most critical task: graciously serving your customers and guests. Think about it! Your role in the organization is absolutely essential, and by wearing your uniform with pride, you wholeheartedly embrace this concept of service.

PROPER FIT AND CLOTHING CARE

When you are required to wear a uniform, there's at least one bonus for you—you save money and are freed from wardrobe planning! But this simplicity still demands that, when you face the world each day, you make certain your appearance and the way you wear your uniform conveys the same quality and care that you put into your performance. Wearing your uniform with class means paying attention to the details such as proper fit, clothing care and the use of accessories.(See pages 102 and 105 for your guide to a professional appearance.)

Proper fit could be described as the relationship between your clothes and your body. When you can breathe and move comfortably—when there is enough space between your body and your clothes—you have achieved perfect fit. A common problem that sabotages many professional people are clothes that are too tight. When I point out to my husband that his clothes are not looking right, he'll say, "The clothes shrank!" And sometimes this is true; our clothes can shrink if washed improperly or too often. But more frequently our bodies have expanded from lack of exercise or overeating. Therefore, we must pay attention to our body's messages; if it needs more "breathing space" to move comfortably, we need to change clothing sizes. When getting your uniform, select a size that fits properly and don't get emotionally attached to a size number. The only person who knows your size is you, but if your uniform looks tight people will notice. Most companies encourage their employees to replace or alter a uniform when necessary.

Clothing care is essential for an impeccable appearance. People will assume that the way you take care of your clothes is the way you perform your job. Attention to clothing details reflects favorably on your performance and, conversely, inattention reflects poorly. Therefore, attend to clothing details—keep your uniform clean and pressed, replace missing buttons, fix falling hems and so forth.

Accessories considered appropriate for your uniform are usually defined by your company. Accessories are those finishing touches that give personal flair to your outfit. A rule of thumb when wearing uniforms is that less is better.

Jewelry should be discreet and not overpower a uniform. For women, earrings should be no larger in size than a nickel or a dime. Dangling earrings are not recommended because they move and interfere with eye contact. Even though men are now wearing earrings, this is not an accessory that is accepted in most business settings. As your hands are one of the tools of your trade, you'll want to keep them neat and uncluttered, and you certainly don't want any jewelry to interfere with your job. One ring per hand— with the exception of combination engagement and wedding rings for women—is considered ideal by most companies; avoid bracelets and bangles.

Your shoes and hose or socks are the foundation of your outfit. Selecting the right style and color and keeping them in good condition is as important as attending to the other pieces of a uniform. Many positions in hospitality require a special type of shoe that allows you to move comfortably and safely. One tip for selecting hose and socks is to choose a color that blends with the two colors next to it. For example, with dark pants, wear dark socks and dark shoes; white socks would provide too much contrast thereby bringing attention to the feet. With a navy or black skirt, select

dark shoes in navy or black and either gray or sheer hose; do not wear ivory or white for the same reason—you do not want too much contrast at the bottom. For more detailed information on selecting the right hose and shoes for the hemline, please see pages 76-77, "Shoes, Hose, Hemlines—The Right Combination."

Now, I invite you to take a look at yourself in front of a long mirror and let's see how your uniform fit and care measure up. Answer the following questions with either "Yes" or "No." Give yourself one point for every "Yes" and add your score. If you can't answer yes to all parts of the question, do not give yourself a point. When you find a question that does not apply to you, give yourself a point anyway, if your answer would theoretically be "Yes."

PROFESSIONAL APPEARANCE CHECKLIST FOR WOMEN

1. Does your blouse fit properly? Do buttons stay closed and not pull across the bust? Does it look loose?
2. If you are wearing a skirt, is it at the knee or below the knee? No creases or pulls across the hips? Can you easily insert two fingers at the waist? Can you turn it around your body?
3. If you are wearing slacks, do they fit properly? Do not wrinkle across the hips? Do pleats remain closed? Do they fall straight from the buttocks?
4. Are your hose in good condition? No runs? Are they in a neutral color? Do they blend with your shoes or hemline?
5. Are your shoes appropriate for your job? Are they in good condition, clean and polished?
6. Is your uniform in excellent condition? No missing buttons, or pulled seams; nothing is torn, stained, discolored or wrinkled?
7. Is your jewelry appropriate for your job? Medium size, classic style, no noisy pieces or dangling earrings?
8. Is your overall appearance neat, clean and appropriate for your job?
9. Are you wearing your name tag on the *right side* of your uniform?
10. Do you look at yourself in a mirror at least three times a day to check your overall appearance and the details?

1

2

3

5

6

4

7

8

1

2

4

3

First Impressions.
The moment that
makes your image.

5

6

7

8

PROFESSIONAL APPEARANCE CHECKLIST FOR MEN

1. Does your shirt fit properly? Can you fit one finger in between the neckline and the collar of the shirt?
2. If your shirt has long sleeves, does the sleeve show one-eighth to one-fourth inches below the jacket sleeve?
3. Does your jacket fit properly? Is it loose enough so that you can button it without horizontal or vertical wrinkles in the back?
4. If you are wearing a tie, does it end at the bottom of the belt buckle?
5. Do your slacks fit you properly? Breaks in the front, falls straight from the buttocks, fits above the stomach and pockets remain closed? Do all these conditions apply to your slacks?
6. Are your slacks long enough so that the hem just touches the top of your shoes?
7. Do your socks match the color of your shoes or your slacks?
8. Are your shoes appropriate for your job?
9. Is your jewelry limited to a watch and one ring per hand?
10. Is your overall look neat, clean and appropriate for your job?
11. Are you wearing your name tag on the *right side* of your uniform?
12. Do you look at yourself in a mirror at least three times a day to check your overall appearance and the details?

How did you score? Women's score _____ Men's score _____

For females the highest score is ten points and for men 12 points. If you had the highest score, congratulations! You can be sure that this part of your appearance is excellent. You are wearing your uniform with pride and care and it shows.

When we conduct the Image Impact seminars, participants fill out these same questionnaires. Then we post the scores on a flip chart to see how the *team's* appearance measures up. Women who score less than ten or men who score less than 12 realize their professional appearance needs some work. Within each question are details on proper fit, clothing care and accessories. Just like our seminar participants, return to those questions where you did not get a point and consider making the necessary changes to score 100 percent! Even a small change will ensure that your appearance supports your career and not limits it.

As you can see, often what makes the big difference in our appearance are the details. One of the reasons why it is important to check yourself in the mirror several times a day is that, after working hard for several hours, some of those important details may need some attention or repair. Using the questionnaire against which to check your uniform daily will assist you in maintaining a well-groomed appearance. Having a high score one day and a low score the next day will not work for you. Remember, you meet people today that you may never see again, and that first impression can positively or negatively influence your career.

A well-groomed appearance is a daily responsibility, as is an excellent job performance. And one affects the other. When we look good, we feel more confident and, therefore, we perform better and get the recognition we deserve. This positive input boosts our self-esteem. Think of how you feel when you get ready for a special social event: Before you leave home, you look yourself over in a mirror and say: "I look good!" Then you go out prepared to have a great time and most of the time you do. That same polished party feeling can be recaptured each and every day when you walk out of your home "bandbox" perfect. When you know you look good, you are ready to face—and enjoy—the day ahead! Such positive expectation is the first step in building your professional image of excellence.

HOSPITALITY:
WHAT YOU SAY—
WHAT YOU DO

$\mathcal{O}$ne of the oldest axioms of human interaction is that the initial impression we make on someone sets the tone for the rest of the relationship. The power of first impressions is that they work both positively and negatively and are very difficult to change. In hospitality we know that guests form their overall impressions of a property during the first ten minutes of their stay—the time it takes the guest to drive up, unload, check in and locate and explore the room. If this first encounter with the property and the staff is pleasant and smooth, the guest senses a feeling of comfort and competence and is inclined to dismiss subsequent problems. By the same token, when any of these first encounters are negative, regardless of subsequent efforts by the hotel employees, the guest is likely to perceive the entire stay as unpleasant. Some companies have created new positions such as "guest service associate" or "guest service assistant." These employees can perform multiple functions from carrying bags, registering or checking out guests, to fielding questions at the front desk. This is an example of how companies are trying to ensure that those critical first ten minutes are positive and pleasant for customers.

Jan Carlzon, former CEO of SAS Airlines, calls these encounters—in which a customer comes into contact with a company and forms an impression—"moments of truth." Because these moments of truth are so difficult to change, we want to ensure that they are positive. And, then, we want to ensure that positive first impression is reinforced with our subsequent crisp and professional appearance, with the way we perform our jobs and by the gracious and courteous way we treat our customers.

Bill Fromm and Keb Schlesinger co-authored *The Real Heroes of Business—and Not a CEO Among Them.* They selected 14 of the finest service workers in our nation from *Fortune* magazine's top 500 service companies and from 300 additional companies. The authors report that these 14 heroes know more about delivering good service than most market researchers and consultants because these people do it every day. One of the key elements they discovered that these 14 had in common is that they see what they do not as jobs, but as roles. They have a sense of obligation to both their own standards as well as to their customers. They see themselves as service performers and have honed dealing with customers to a fine art—one that carefully balances the needs of the customers with those of the business. When someone chooses to work in hospitality, we assume that they have a natural ability to work with people and they derive satisfaction and joy from being of service. It is very difficult, if not downright impossible, to ask someone who does not feel comfortable with people to perform well in a service business like hospitality.

Jack Whelan, a business traveler who stays in hotels 125 nights a year, was selected by *USA Today* to pose as a hospitality employee for several days. During this experiment, he checked in passengers at an airline and at a large city hotel; he delivered room service, made beds, toted luggage, cleaned toilets and checked guests in and out at the front desk. After his experience, he concluded: "It can be pretty hard to meet the service level that the customers are looking for. I don't care if you are a college-educated Ph.D.; it takes a certain amount of skill. It takes an attitude." When he was told the credo of the hotel he had worked at, "Every guest leaves satisfied," he nodded in agreement; but he also recognized that things go wrong. "This service stuff isn't easy. You can't fake it!"

In this chapter, we will explore the attributes and behaviors that excellent service workers perform every day with ease and delight, making hospitality a fun, challenging and rewarding profession. We will show how to make our body language convey the same messages of excellent service as do our actions and words. We will share the key words used in hospitality that are considered *magic* because of the delightful effect they have on a guest. We will explain how our voice enhances or conflicts with our spoken words. Our appearance and grooming are the first steps to setting the stage for a best impression. This chapter will provide you with the tools to continue building on that first and lasting impression as well as to make your job easier, more interesting and fun!

YOUR BODY SPEAKS

The words we speak, hear, read and write are only a small part of the way we communicate with one another. In face-to-face encounters, most of what we communicate is done without speaking a word. Non-verbal communication is everything we don't say; it is our body language, how we act and react and what we convey to others when we are with them. If you really want to communicate sincere desire and commitment to serve your guests and clients, you must put your entire self into your interactions—posture, facial expressions, body position, movement, gestures, tone of voice and attitudes. The body does not know how to lie!

Have you ever asked a loved one *"Are you OK?"* because you knew just by looking at him or her that something was wrong and yet you got the response that *"Yes! Everything is fine!"*? In this case, the words are saying one thing but the body and the voice are saying something different. In a now well-known study, Albert Mehrabian, UCLA psychologist, found that when there is a perceived conflict between verbal messages and emotional content, then the implicit behavior has more weight than the words. He says, "In the realm of feelings, our facial and vocal expressions, postures, movements and gestures are so important that when our words contradict the messages contained within them, others mistrust what we say—they rely almost completely on what we do."

Other people's perceptions of our message could be weighted this way: 7% verbal (the words we choose), 38% vocal feeling and 55% facial expressions. Therefore, we need to pay attention to our body language to ensure that it is supporting our verbal messages.

MAINTAIN YOUR POSTURE

Our posture—the way we stand, walk and sit—sends immediate messages to others. An upright body sends a message of competence, pride and confidence. If we slump over with our shoulders slack, we send a message of vulnerability which in most people's minds is linked to uncertainty, uneasiness and laziness. Walking straight with your head held high sends the signal that you own your space and you have the right to be there. People who scuff along, head down, signal dejection. Moving easily, not cautiously, standing and sitting upright and getting up and sitting down with ease, all contribute to a youthful image, an image of vigor and strength. My mother is a great example of vigorous posture. She walks and stands like a young woman even though she's over 70; she said that when she was young she learned how to walk tall by putting a phone book on her head and walking around the living room. Even today, if anyone in our family is slumping, she'll admonish us to "Stand up straight dear!"

In his book, *Subtext—Making Body Language Work in the Workplace,* Julius Fast says that women need to be aware of the way they carry their upper body. With shoulders pitched forward and the chest pulled in and minimized, the subtext is "I am ashamed of my body" which makes it impossible to signal confidence and certainty. We remind women in our seminars that if they lean on anything when standing, they lose 90 percent of their power. With men, the middle part of the body is the vulnerable area. When a man tightens his abdomen and lets these muscles pull in his stomach, he's sending a strong message that "I am aware of you."

Maintaining good posture takes some work, but it is necessary in order to look more alert, eager and energetic. It also gives you the energy it takes to physically perform a demanding job like yours. When standing, keep your weight balanced over your center of gravity: feet solidly planted on the ground, legs slightly apart and arms straight down at your sides relaxed and without stiffness. Keep your rib cage off your hips, your head straight yet loose, your eyes level, your chin down and your stomach in. This posture conveys respect for our guests as we remain alert and ready to attend to their needs and wants.

TOO CLOSE FOR COMFORT

Effective professional people act as if they "own" their space. Your professional space is where you perform your job, whether it is an office, the entrance of a property, a laundry room, a tool room, a kitchen or a front desk. You own this space through erect posture, assertive movements and a "host" behavior which is expressed, for example, by greeting "outsiders" who enter your work space. Having respect for others' "private" space is also essential in relating well to others. That private space is the "bubble" or the "comfort zone" in which every person feels comfortable and will not allow others to enter without permission. In the United States, England and Germany, people prefer a two-foot bubble of space around them. When two people talk, the "bubbles" touch, and there is a four-foot distance that is considered the best distance for conversation or business discussions. If you stand or sit further away, you may seem cold and aloof. If you get closer, your nearness may feel like intimidation or invasion which will also inhibit the communication. Only loved ones or helpers are allowed in that private space. For example, when we help someone carry luggage, put on their coat or serve them food, this closeness is not considered an invasion. For the Japanese, though, a one-arm-length distance between two people in a business encounter is perceived as too close. Their cultural norm is double or triple the distance at which Americans comfortably talk. In contrast, French, Italians, Latin Americans and Eastern Europeans like to stand close and they often touch one another. Being aware of these differences will increase your ability to communicate and establish rapport with your clients and guests. You do not have to adopt their spacing patterns. On the other hand, be sensitive to their reactions and allow space when desired, and don't be offended if someone comes "too close."

Getting too close makes most people uncomfortable, inhibiting communication.

Respecting "personal space" makes most people comfortable.

THE POWER OF A SMILE

Studies at Yale University show that the most important factor in determining whether you impress others favorably when you are trying to come across as persuasive, is *how often you smile*. Nothing else carries as much weight. In hospitality, smiling is a natural way of communicating an attitude of good cheer and making people feel welcome. Smiles draw attention to you and make others feel at ease. One of the large hotel chains, when selecting employees from a large number of applicants, excluded candidates who smiled fewer than four times during the interview. In one of our seminars on "Gracious Hospitality," one of the participants asked how often she needed to smile during the day; "It gets tiring," she said. Another participant responded: "It is necessary to smile at least once during every new encounter with a guest; besides, it must come natural to you without effort." For a hospitality professional, smiling is like painting for a painter; it comes naturally, easy and gives you joy.

Smiling also is an instant energizer; it make you look more approachable, friendly, relaxed, open and comfortable. It shows others that you have a sense of well-being and that you enjoy life. In addition, smiling improves your voice quality by relaxing your throat muscles, and it takes fewer facial muscles to smile than to frown. It also makes you look younger. A smile is your most important communication accessory!

The most valuable message of eye contact is "recognition."

EFFECTIVE EYE CONTACT

If you want your interactions to be congenial and productive, always start by looking the other person in the eye. We have mentioned that eye contact is one of the most powerful tools we have in hospitality. Looking a person in the eye means that we acknowledge their presence and for that moment they are the most important person to us. It also sends a very attentive, supporting message: "I'm listening to every word." Failing to make eye contact sends the disturbing message that "I do not meet your eye because to me you are not there, you are a non-person, insignificant." The most valuable message of eye contact is *recognition*. A fleeting glance is not enough; penetrate, bond, create mutual attention and readiness. In most instances, eye contact lasts only about a second before one of the parties looks away. Your initial gaze, if you are the one that initiates the encounter, should be fairly long, perhaps two or three seconds and concentrated. Be careful not to stare at people which could be intimidating and make them uncomfortable. Break eye contact frequently as you talk or listen. The best technique is to look down to the side, and then back. One of the values of eye contact is to assure the other person that we are listening to them. A polite listener will focus on the chin, mouth, or one side of the other person's face.

Remember also that the rules of eye contact vary from culture to culture. In our culture, prolonged eye contact is too disturbing, just as a refusal to make eye contact is considered rude. In other cultures, particularly in Latin America, eye contact is linked to status. The Japanese tend to avoid eye contact, considering it impolite and intimidating.

Lack of eye contact makes people feel ignored and non-existent.

GESTURES ACROSS CULTURES

"Successful people get ahead by using their heads—intellectually and physically," says D.A Benton in her book *Lions Don't Need to Roar.* They have relaxed/ready facial expressions, smile, keep a level head, occasionally and purposely nod, rather than incessantly bob their heads; of course, they maintain eye contact as well as use their eyes to help them communicate effectively. Simply holding your head level may seem trivial or insignificant, but it is a subtle behavior than can say a lot about you. When your head is level, you look more in control and sure of yourself; you appear more energetic and are in a better position to give others valuable eye contact.

Stiff postures, tensed muscles, clenched fists and pursed lips come across as threatening. The other person tends to react in kind by stiffening up. When you are under stress, your body gestures often put others on guard, even if unintentionally. We all know the clues: A raised eyebrow communicates surprise; a wink conveys sly agreement or alliance; tightly set lips signal opposition. Your arms should be held loosely at your sides as a sign of openness. Putting your hands over your mouth sends a message of embarrassment, of hiding something or shows a reluctance to speak which makes it difficult for guests to approach you for help. Chewing a pencil, other object or gum, besides being improper and impolite, signals nervousness or anger. Traditionally, someone who sits with arms and legs in an open posture sends a signal of being receptive to new ideas and suggestions. Closed arms and legs may indicate disagreement even though a woman wearing a skirt will, of course, choose to close her legs regardless of her attitude. If you lean back in your chair to listen to someone, this posture may be interpreted as showing a lack of interest in the other person. Leaning forward signals intensity and interest. If you find yourself in a conversation with two people sandwiched on either side of you, it is difficult to pay attention to them both. You may want to turn part of your body to one person and the rest to the other person. Incline your head to the one on your right while the rest of your body faces left. From time to time, alternate positions. This effort show that you are interested in what both of them are saying.

Gestures that have clear, unambiguous significance in our culture can mean something different to foreigners. Psychology professors Paul Ekman and Wallace V. Friesen from the University of California have identified several gestures that can get business people in trouble. These include:

- The "A-Okay" sign (thumb held to forefinger to make a ring) means "That's great" in the United States, but in France and

Belgium it means "You are worth zero." And in Greece and Turkey it's an invitation for sex or a vulgar insult.

- The "thumbs up" gesture does not mean "good" or "all right" for everyone. In Northern Greece, Sardinia and elsewhere, it conveys a vulgar meaning.
- Nodding the head up and down means "yes" in the United States and most other countries. In Greece and Turkey, however, it can mean "no" if the head is tilted high or if the nodding is accompanied by a clicking of the tongue.

When dealing with guests and clients from other cultural backgrounds, be aware of their gestures without judgment and go easy on your own gestures. The safest policy to establish rapport with people from all cultures is not to use gestures at all. You do not want to take the risk of being misinterpreted. The universal gestures of good posture, an open, sincere smile, serene facial expression, free unrestrained movements and effective eye contact will carry silent messages of interest and respect that will be appreciated and well interpreted by all.

THE MAGIC WORDS

Some of the things you can do to provide excellent service are relatively simple and easy, such as choosing your language carefully. When we refer to our customers we mean not only the guests and clients that visit our properties, but also our coworkers and managers who are part of the team. Whether we are communicating with *external customers* (guests, clients, suppliers) or *internal customers* (coworkers, managers), the words we use significantly impact the way we interact with those we serve and work with.

Using *I* instead of *they* or *we* is critical to conveying your commitment to the other person. To a customer, the company begins and ends with you; therefore, when you use the word *I* it tells them that you assume the responsibility for taking care of the customer in the name of the entire company. Using *I* shows that you understand and accept full responsibility such as in *"I'm sorry you had to wait that long,"* or *"How may I help you?"*

Let's look at the seven *Magic Words:*

1. Greetings

People will remember what you tell them at the beginning and at the end of an encounter. Acknowledging a customer's presence with eye contact, a smile and the proper greeting shows the customer that they are welcome and that we have acknowledged their presence. Many times in our daily interaction with guests, coworkers and friends, we use greetings such as *Hi!, Hi there!,* or *Hello!,* which become so mechanical that these expressions lose their real meaning. Besides, these expressions are too casual for some guests. Americans tend to be a more casual, informal society, which is not always appreciated by other cultures that tend to see this treatment as a lack of respect. The appropriate greeting with a courteous happy tone of voice and saying it as if you mean it, will bring a smile to your customer's face:

> Good morning!
> Good afternoon!
> Good evening!

If you know the person's name, use it; it will make them feel very welcome and recognized.

2. "How may I help you?"

When expressing the willingness to help a customer, most of us use the expression: *"May I help you?"* This common expression is called a *closed-ended* question, and it calls for a *"Yes"* or a *"No"* answer. After the person responds *"No thanks!"* that marks the end of the encounter. If the answer is *"Yes!,"* then either you have to ask another question, such as, *"What can I do for you?,"* or the other person will automatically tell you how you can help them. Using the *open-ended* question, *"How may I help you?,"* makes a big difference. We assume that you can always help them; you just need to know what kind of help you can offer at this time. This form of expression opens the door for the customer to easily express his or her need, making the communication clear, quick and to the point.

3. "PLEASE..."

The word *please* is a mandatory, courteous expression for people who interact in either social or work situations. Used to make a polite request, it also helps to secure the other person's attention. *"Yes, please"* means that "Yes, I accept and I am grateful." It also can be used to turn a question into a request; for example: Asking a customer *"Could you wait for a few minutes, please?"* is different than *"Could you wait for a few minutes?"* The latter is just a question, meaning "Is it possible?" Adding *"please"* to ask others for more time, documents, favors, patience, understanding or any other thing required in the daily process of service, is a gentle way of showing respect and asking for understanding.

4. "THANK YOU!"

In hospitality we need to say *"Thanks!"* to everyone after every encounter. We need to give *thanks to our customers* when they do business with us. Customers have many options for the kind of service we provide. It is easy to take our regular customers for granted, but we cannot afford to do that. Saying thanks for doing business with us reminds them that we value the gift of business they bring to our company. Say *"Thank you"* to your customers:

- When they compliment you or the company; accepting a positive compliment gracefully is a sign of professionalism.
- When they offer comments or suggestions—it shows that you value their feedback and opinions.
- When they are patient...and not so patient. It helps diffuse the discomfort of waiting which no one likes anyway.
- When they help you serve them better. It shows you appreciate them taking the effort to provide you with information or other assistance that makes your life a lot easier.
- When they complain to you. A complaint gives you the chance to correct a problem and a second chance to serve them better.

Remember to say *thank you* to:
- *Your coworkers,* who help you to do your job. Hospitality is truly team work and we want to thank the team members.
- *Your supervisor.* Giving positive feedback to managers helps you to receive the support you need to perform your job.
- *Your vendors,* who provide you with the supplies and services which allow you to give outstanding service to your customers.
- *Yourself!* Give yourself the credit you deserve for a job well done. Every time another person says *"Thanks"* to you, extend the same gratitude to yourself and reward yourself with something special once in a while.

5. "IT'S MY PLEASURE!"

When finishing an encounter, express your sincere feelings for having the opportunity of making that encounter a pleasant one. You may use your creativity to express these positive feelings. Some companies invite their employees to use expressions such as: *"It is always my pleasure!"* or *"It is a pleasure"* or *"You are very welcome!"* You want to finish the communication on a positive note, reminding others that your joy is to make them happy; that, indeed, it is your purpose to have the opportunity to fulfill their needs and wants. People who are hospitable enjoy seeing others happy. That is the true meaning of hospitality.

6. "I'M SORRY."

These words—*"I'm sorry"*—are so simple and they are not used frequently enough. The solution to every problem, whether major or minor in hospitality, should start with a sincere apology. Many people find it hard to say *"I'm sorry"* and maybe that's because they think they have failed or that they were not professional enough. But this is not true. An apology is simply an acknowledgment that things are not going right in your customer's eyes, and recognizing it opens the door for correction.

For an apology to be effective, it must be sincere, personal and timely. A vague apology expressed in an impersonal, robot-like manner, can be worse than no apology at all. Expressing our sincere concern for the customer's feelings is important and we must make them personal. Here again, the use of the word *I* instead of *We* or *They* is critical. It means we take responsibility for the problem even if it is not a result of our behavior. In the eyes of the customer, you are the company at all times and especially when something goes wrong. The sooner we react to the distressed customer, the better. Do not wait until you find the source or cause of the problem; this is not important to the customer. They want to know that we acknowledge that there is a problem and that we are going to solve it.

7. "I'LL BE HAPPY TO..."

Many times we get reasonable and *unreasonable* requests from customers. Other times we offer additional services and touches that make the customer feel not only satisfied but delighted. *"I'll be happy to..."* conveys the message that we can do the expected and the unexpected and that we have fun in doing so. Giving an additional extra service without these words, is like giving a painting without the frame. Besides, you want to verbally make your customers aware that you are going the extra mile for them. Even when you provide a service to fulfill a common expectation, your action has more value in the eyes of your customers if you do it with enjoyment. *"I'll be happy to..."* is an effective response to a customer's request.

8. NAMES

> *"Remember that a person's name is, to him/her,*
> *the sweetest and most important sound*
> *in any language."* DALE CARNEGIE

People want to hear their names—and often—to feel that they are getting personalized service. It is, of course, important to use the correct name. Always call your customers by their last name; for example: Mr. or Mrs. Miller instead of Bill or Rose. When customers want to be called by their first names, they will let you know. Calling them by their first names without their invitation is considered rude. It is appropriate to begin an encounter in a formal mode and go informal if and when the customer lets us know. When you have difficulty pronouncing a customer's last name, it is appropriate to ask for assistance. As a foreigner in the United States, I have a hard time with the pronunciation of many last names. When I ask people *"Could you please help me to pronounce your name correctly?"* they respond happily to my request. People appreciate your desire to say their names correctly. There are many ways of obtaining the guests' and clients' names so you can use them in your communications. In our seminars, employees of all positions discuss the different, creative ways to find out guests' names. Some of our participants have mentioned sources such as: luggage tags, credit cards, computer listings and so forth. Take a few minutes and think of ways in your job position that you can learn the names of the guests you come in contact with.

Remembering names and using them in your encounters is a skill that can be developed by anyone who makes the effort. All the service providers written about in *The Real Heroes of Business* had one quality in common: They always use the names of their customers when serving them. Here is a quick formula to help you develop or increase this valuable skill:

1. Prepare to hear or find out the name; pay attention!
2. Repeat the name immediately. If necessary, ask the person to repeat it or to spell it out, or you spell it out and ask for confirmation.
3. Make a mental association: Look for something funny or special about either the person or the name. One tip is to relate part of the name to a facial feature. Example: You meet Samuel Keyes and he has a proportionally small mouth; imagine the dentist opening his mouth with a pair of keys. If the guest does not have a prominent feature, make up a silly story. Picture Mr. Keyes as a modern day Ben Franklin flying a kite with two keys in a storm. Make a game of this and it will be fun!
4. Use the name more than once in an encounter without overdoing it.
5. Use the name again at the end of the encounter: "Mr. Spencer, come and see us again!"

9. Your favorite

The last magic word belongs to you. Take a few minutes and think of an expression that is part of your daily work life that has elicited a good response from those you work with. Let me share my favorite. I only noticed that I use it because some of my clients pointed it out to me and told me how much they appreciated it: When anyone asks me if they can use something that I have, I usually reply: *"Please, be my guest."* What is yours? _____

Words to Avoid

Words are very powerful and they can elicit both good and bad reactions from our customers. Just as the *Magic Words* will bring a smile to your customers' faces, there are other words that will create an immediate negative reaction. Nancy Friedman, known as the "Phone Doctor," shares some phrases that can intentionally or unintentionally create anger and frustration in our customers:

Avoid	Use Instead
• *"I don't know"*	"Let me check to find out"
• *"We can't do that"*	"Let's see what we can do" and, then, find an alternative solution.
• *"You will have to"*	"You may (or will) need to"; "Here is how we can help you with that" or "Next time that happens, here is what we can do."
• *"NO!" when used at the beginning of a sentence*	Think before you speak and turn the answer into a positive response: "We aren't able to but this is what we can do."

There is another expression that is commonly used in service that has a double meaning: *"No problem!"* When we say *"No prob-*

lem," we are assuming that the guest's request is a problem and that we will make it disappear or minimize it. A more positive response could be *"Certainly!,"* or, alternatively, use one the phrases mentioned before, such as *"I'll be happy to!,"* or *"It'll be my pleasure!"* or *"Consider it done!"*

The list of the words and expressions that can create a negative response in either internal or external customers does not stop here. Many times we send negative messages to others using expressions that we don't consider negative, but are perceived this way. Also, when we "talk down" to customers—like we might talk to a small child—we create the same reaction. Phrases such as "Do you understand?" could mean "I think you are stupid!" Instead, you could check if your explanation was understood without making your customer feel stupid by asking *"I want to be sure that I explained this to you correctly"* or *"I want to check that you have all the information on this."* Now, take a few minutes and make a list of those words and phrases that either you or your coworkers have found make your customers angry or upset. This list, in addition to the *magic words* list, will help you to select only those words that convey a message of hospitality and service to your customers.

YOUR VOICE IS SAYING . . . .

One major city hotel conducted a "secret guest research" to evaluate how the employees were performing different guest-related functions within the property. One thing they discovered was that some employees, when showing the guests to their rooms, were describing perfectly all the characteristics and amenities of the rooms, but they sounded like they were reading a script in a monotonous voice. This emotionless script sounded impersonal to the guest, which was more unpleasant than if the employee had made a mistake in the content. In this case, the words were appropriate in showing and welcoming someone into a room, but *the tone of voice was saying something different.* The message that the guest perceived was something like: *"This is what I am supposed to tell you and I am tired of saying it one more time."* In this case, the voice, the tone, the pace and no pauses made these encounters unpleasant to the customers.

The *Magic Words* mentioned above will only produce a smile and pleasant response in your guests if they come not only from your head—your memory—but also from your heart. Think of the way you welcome friends and loved ones into your own home; think of the way you greet them and help them to settle into their rooms and how you take care of them at the dinner table and how you are willing to help them in any way you can to make their stay a pleasant one. In the same way, working in hospitality is extending ourselves and putting our heart into it every time we interact with a guest. It is true that after many hours on the job, things may get monotonous and we are tempted to use the same words in a tired voice. The good news is that our mind can help us in moments of tiredness: When you approach or meet your fifth, your 50th or your 500th customer of the day, think for a moment that, although you have attended to many just like this one, to this person you are employee *Number One!* You may be the first, only or last employee that customer will talk and interact with. This thought will help your mind, your body and your voice speak to this person with a different attitude.

With a little effort and a few simple changes, you can develop a voice that helps you better control how you affect others. The first thing you must learn or relearn is how to breathe correctly! When speech therapists work with a public speaker, the first and most important lessons are related to breathing. Once we relearn to breath as deeply and slowly as we should, it increases the flow of oxygen to our brain thereby improving our thinking process. In addition, it reduces muscle tension and improves the quality of our voice. Breathing correctly calms your spirit and your mind, improves circulation and reminds us to relax our facial expressions. The key to correct breathing is to breathe from your abdomen with your diaphragm pushing air up and out instead of breathing from your throat.

For a more effective voice:

- *Use your entire body when you speak.* Your body and facial expressions enhance the effect of anything your say. Think of the message you want to convey and say it with your words, your voice, your body and put your heart into it!

- *Start each new thought with a new breath of air.* Also, save enough breath or take a second one to end your thought with power and emphasis. Sometimes it will be more effective to begin quietly and build so that the last words get more emphasis.
- *Speak slowly.* Hurrying makes our words less important and gives the impression that we do not think that what we are saying deserves more than a brief moment. Slow down. Allow for some pauses, some silence. People will listen more closely and have more respect for what they hear.

Here is a tip for projecting a friendly and courteous voice when you feel tired. Let's do this simple exercise now: Please make a frown and with your eyebrows as close together as possible, as if you are very upset, say: *"Good Morning!"* Did you hear the tone of your voice? Now, relax the muscles of your face and with no facial expression, repeat: *"Good Morning!"* Did you hear a difference? Now, open your face and raise your eyebrows even if you look funny and say: *"Good Morning!"* Did you hear the tone of your voice? It should sound pleasant as if you were smiling! When you raise your eyebrows, your face opens, the muscles of your throat stretch and open up in such a way that the vocal cords produce a pleasant sound, even if you do not intend to do so. So, raise your eyebrows when you need to boost your voice to welcome that guest for whom you are employee *Numero Uno!*

To avoid sounding monotonous when reciting something you say many times each day, use a *pause.* By pausing and breathing in between your sentences, you will sound different, and your tone of voice will change making your description more interesting. Pay attention to your tone of voice, volume, pace, tone, inflection and your breathing to ensure that the message you are sending to your customers is consistent and both your words and your voice are saying the same thing.

YOUR ACTIONS COUNT

In hospitality excellence means serving and delighting our customers. It implies doing our job at a high standard of quality and delivering it with a warm and caring attitude. "Consistent, high quality service boils down to two equally important things: caring and competence," says Chip R. Bell and Ron Zemke in their book *Service Wisdom*. Excellence in hospitality goes beyond doing things for the client's comfort; it also includes a caring feeling and expressing that caring in a way that makes a difference.

In an era of flattened hierarchies and heightened expectations, hospitality performers that excel are those who are resilient and resourceful, empathetic and enterprising, competent and creative— a set of skills that are no longer demanded from managers only. Regardless of your position in the company, whether you are serving internal or external customers, the adage that "Actions speak louder than words" applies to service excellence. Generally speaking, others weigh our actions more than our words as they try to understand what we feel. Internal and external customers know that they can trust you because of the competence and confidence you display in your work. It is your commitment to quality that assures customer satisfaction and good relations with coworkers.

Following are some of the key actions that demonstrate your competence and your caring attitude to the customer.

LISTEN

Good communications in customer relations requires not only the skill of talking but the ability to *listen*. Many studies show that listening actually consumes more of our workday than talking, yet very seldom do we receive training in how to listen effectively. Effective listening helps us to understand what the customer wants so we can fulfill and exceed their expectations. It also prevents misunderstanding and mistakes and it builds long-term relationships. Think of your favorite friend and those professionals you always prefer; they are the people who *really listen to you*. The same is true for our customers. Effective listening is more than having eye contact and keeping our mouth closed. It includes closing down your own internal dialogue to hear what the customer is really saying. Here are some tips for effective listening:

- Look at the other person with a relaxed, open facial expression and occasionally nod or say "uh-huh."

- Pay attention to the content.
- Listen completely at first. Try to get every nuance of meaning available and encourage the other person to continue by saying something like: "Tell me more," or "Anything else?" Try to really understand.
- Resist the temptation to jump in and speak as soon as the other person pauses or takes a break. Give the other person the "air time" they need.
- For clarity, repeat what you hear. Paraphrasing or summarizing the points gives the other person the opportunity to clear up misunderstandings. You may even ask: "Is this what you meant?"
- Do not interrupt. If you catch yourself interrupting inappropriately, immediately apologize and let the other person continue. One interruption can be considered an accident. Two or three is irritating and damages the communication process.

Never underestimate the value of listening to your customers. It's one of the most valuable skills you can learn. Do you want a good description of the word *listen?* If you like to play with letters, rearrange the six letters that compose this word and you get the true meaning of *listen = silent!*

KNOW YOUR JOB AND MORE...

Customers expect that we perform our job with mastery. Mastery of the job for a *hospitality professional* includes understanding our customers' needs and satisfying them to the best of our abilities. It also implies our commitment to learn how we can serve them better. It is not a final state; it is a continuous process that changes and improves according to our customers' needs and wants. Mastering our job for the customer includes fulfilling their needs and expectations with *efficiency* and *speed.* It means a job well done, at the highest quality and without waste of time or resources. Timing is critical since one minute of wait time can seem like ten minutes to your customer. Your job knowledge includes:

- *The ability to answer questions.* Customers expect you to know more than the limits of your particular job. At a given moment, you represent the company for a customer and they expect that either you will provide what they need or that you will guide them to someone within the organization that can fulfill their needs. This decade's theory of "employee empowerment" has given employees more resources and creativity to fulfill customers' requests.

- *Knowing where things are.* It is very common that whether you are in sales, housekeeping, management, security or any other position for that matter, you are continually asked questions such as: "Where is the restaurant?" "Where can I make a phone call?", and so forth. Customers will ask you about where things are located not only at the property but outside the property as well. Answering these questions yourself or directing the customer to those people who can answer them puts you at the top of service excellence. Here is when a response of *"I don't know"* will upset your guests. Having enough information about the organization and how it operates will enable you to guide the customer to the right person and to the right place to fulfill their needs.

- *Solving problems without delay.* Customers do not expect you to be perfect, but they do expect you to fix things when they go wrong without delay. When something goes wrong, an *apology* is the first step in the "recovery process;" the process also includes *listening with empathy* to their problem and then *fixing the problem quickly.* The sense of urgency that you take when solving a customer's problem tells them that you really care and that you are committed to finding a solution. If you can *provide some value-added gesture* that says "I want to make it up to you" this will convert an unsatisfied customer to a grateful one when we have not lived up to their expectations. More than once I have received a complete dinner with additional dessert "on the house" because of unusually slow service. I still go back to those restaurants because I believe in their usual great service. Then, the last step in the recovery process which sometimes is forgotten: *follow up* to be sure that what you have "fixed" really worked for the guest. Do not assume that things are corrected exactly as you thought they would be. Check to be sure. It gives you a second chance to show the customer your commitment to their satisfaction. When a poor service performance is rescued with skill, you can actually impress a customer more than with ordinary service and can turn a casual customer into a regular customer.

Most employees today have the power to make things right for customers who are miffed about service. The risk of losing a customer is very costly. Some companies limit how much you can take off from customers' bills to ensure their satisfaction. "Any decision that you make that makes guests happy when they leave is the right decision," says one hotel manager to his employees. By following your company's policy and using common sense and creativity, you will find ways to make things right for your customers.

DELIVERING PROMISES

Our customers receive many promises about our services. Some of them come from the organization and some come from you. Look at the marketing and advertising materials that your company sends to the public. These are some of the promises companies offer in their publicity:

- "We deliver world-class customer service."
- "What sets us apart are the dedicated people who not only fulfill your needs, but anticipate them—people who respond promptly to any request, at any hour."
- "You will see our employees go out of their way to make sure your stay is extraordinary."
- "You will have as a result, a flawless meeting experience."
- "You will love the stay, you will love the service!"
- "When it comes to gourmet cuisine, you will not find any more healthful than ours—whether impeccably served in a banquet setting, in one of our restaurants or in your room."

These promises bring customers to our doors. People select our property based on these promises. However, the majority of the customer promises comes from you. These are the daily promises you make to the customer while performing your job: "Your room will be ready in 30 minutes;" "The projector will be in the room by five this evening;" "I'll send the budget for your wedding reception by Monday." Just think of all the promises you make daily while performing your job to both internal and external customers. When delivering your promises, it is important that you do *what* you promised, *when* you promised. Again, there are no shortcuts—you do whatever it takes to deliver what you promised and in the time frame you promised. You are responsible for the new expectations the customer has based on your promise. Many people make the mistake of giving unrealistic or very tight timetables to customers thinking that this will satisfy them. It could backfire. When the service is not provided in the time that the customer expected, this creates dissatisfaction. But if you add a "cushion" of additional time to what you really expect fulfilling the service to take and then deliver early, the customer will be pleasantly surprised with your promptness. Example: Room service takes 15 minutes. When you tell the guest that breakfast will be in the room in 15 minutes and it takes 17 minutes, the guest is unhappy that it took longer than promised. If you tell the guest that breakfast will be there in 20 or 25 minutes, and the service person knocks at the guest's door in 17 minutes, then the reaction is "Bravo! How fast!" It's the same delivery but it creates different reactions in the guest; the only difference was the expectations you created. In some situations (not always), you can control the expectations you create in your customer when you make promises. Be good to yourself; if you can give yourself some leeway, do so; not only can you prevent delays but you can convert the ordinary into the extraordinary.

REMEMBER: *The organization's promises are what bring the customers to the door. The way you deliver the organization's promises and your own promises is what brings the customers back.*

THE EXTRA MILE IS NEVER CROWDED

The surest way to delight our customers and make them want to come back over and over again, is to practice the "and some more" principle. It is the willingness to go the extra mile that separates the true champions from the also-rans. Napoleon Hill, author of the famous book *Think and Grow Rich,* studied the reasons why some people succeed and so many fail. He researched the lives of many great achievers in many fields. One of his best recommendations to those who want to succeed is to cultivate the habit of "rendering more and better service than that for which you are paid." He recommends this for two reasons: First, it puts you head and shoulders above the competition because most people only provide the minimum service required. Regardless of your position in the organization, when you provide more of what you are supposed to and you perform it better than others, it puts you on the road to excellence. Second, you will build an outstanding reputation as an employee and as a person. Your customers will value and appreciate your service, asking for you whenever they return and expressing their appreciation for your efforts. You will also become a team player whose efforts will be noticed and rewarded by coworkers and managers.

Take just a few moments to reflect on those situations in which you have gone the extra mile for your coworkers and for your customers. Remember the most challenging ones and the funny ones. You can probably replicate now the personal satisfaction you felt then and the appreciation that you received. During our seminars on hospitality, we invite our participants to share some of those *extra mile* experiences with the group. Regardless of the part of the country, participants teach me great lessons on service excellence. I am amazed at their creativity and their willingness to go out of their way to solve the impossible and to do things beyond their line of duty for their customers.

Those special touches—the additional services that are not part of your job description, the things that your internal and external customers do not expect, the things that amaze others and make them remember you—are all part of the extra mile. Research in hospitality has found that these *little* and *not so little things* make the *big difference* between service and service excellence. The commitment to excellence to go the extra mile is something that no one can ask you to do, pay you for doing or make you do. It has to come from within—from your heart—when you realize the great value of your role in the organization. It is the natural result of feeling a vital part of the team and owning the mission of your company as *yours*. When you see and feel this commitment, going the extra mile comes naturally to you without effort. It is the spirit behind the job skills that motivate us to go the extra mile, to perform the impossible and to reach beyond our perceived limits. The need to give to others, the passion for solving problems, the personal gratification of making others' life easier and pleasant are some of the underlying motives that sustain us in our work. Bobbie Gee says it beautifully in her book, *Winning the Image Game*: "The highest skill level in customer relations is the ability to touch that inner need to feel important. This is where the emotional connection takes place and loyal customers are created. Despite the rarity of this skill, it is not difficult to practice and master." Let this rare way of relating become your way of life; you will see that what you put out always comes back to you multiplied. Life rewards those who give!

BUSINESS ETIQUETTE: CHARMING THE BOTTOM LINE

*T*oday good manners is good business. Proper etiquette and manners are considered key elements of quality service. A survey of the top Fortune 500 companies found that 80 percent of the presidents, vice-presidents and chief executive officers had impeccable manners and were self-confident in all encounters. However, when middle management was surveyed that percentage dropped to 40. And among the young, newly hired managers only 12 percent were so skilled. Clearly, there is room for improvement in this area because in today's business environment we are expected to be as self-assured in the social aspects of our business as we are in the technical side.

Managers and those professionals who are climbing the hospitality career ladder face many situations requiring social skills. Business is conducted not only in offices and in boardrooms, but at social gatherings, conventions and at the dinner table. The challenge is that in today's business environment much of the social and business graciousness that worked before is no longer current. Not all social behavior can be transferred exactly to the business setting. Most women want and expect different treatment at the office than they do in social situations. We now communicate through car phones, cellular phones and by fax, voice mail and E-mail. There is confusion about what is the proper and considerate way to treat each other—whether in person or through a machine—and this confusion affects our confidence. Some managers have expressed their concern about how to conduct proper introductions at a meeting, whether to extend their hands to female clients or wait for them to initiate the handshake and many other issues that distract them from conducting business.

Confidence comes from knowledge, observation and practice. It comes from knowing what to do, when to do it and doing it with sophistication. Sophistication is not something that you are born with; it is something that you learn and cultivate. Even if you were born with the proverbial silver spoon in your mouth, you may have discovered that you do not necessarily have all the answers. Our work environment is changing so rapidly that we need to be flexible and attentive to the new, appropriate behaviors.

This chapter will provide you with the guidelines of how to behave in those social and business situations that are common to the hospitality professional—whether it is at the office, at a social gathering, at the dinner table, through a telecommunication device or at the boardroom. Learning the new rules of etiquette and manners will let you handle any situation with ease and confidence. Your etiquette and manners will become a key strategy to getting ahead and staying ahead in the business world so you will navigate in the '90s with confidence and class.

YOUR ETIQUETTE IQ

Etiquette and manners are the social or human side of business. Etiquette is a blend of poise, self-confidence, control and style that can empower us to command respect in any situation. When situations offer several behavior options and we don't know the right thing to do, we feel awkward. Letitia Baldrige, author of the *Complete Guide to Executive Manners,* says that *"Good manners consist of two thirds of logic and common sense and one third of kindness."*

You may want to test your "Etiquette IQ" by answering these questions:

1. Your boss, Ms. Brown, enters the room where you are meeting with Mr. Anderson, an important client. You stand and say: "Ms. Brown, I want to introduce Mr. Anderson our client from Chicago." Is your introduction correct?

Yes ___ No ___

2. A man has been introduced to a woman at a business meeting. He reaches out to shake her hand saying: "Hello." Is he correct?

Yes ___ No ___

3. A visitor enters the room. What should you do?
   a. Remain seated if you are a woman
   b. Stand and remain standing until the visitor is seated
   c. Stand if you are a man since only men need to stand

4. When riding in an elevator with a woman, a man should always allow the woman to exit first.

Yes __ No ___

5. During a business meal, you need to leave the table for a few minutes. What do you do with your napkin?
   a. Leave it on the table neatly folded
   b. Place it on the right side of your plate loosely folded
   c. Leave it on your chair
   d. Take it with you

6. During a luncheon meeting, what is the appropriate amount to drink?
   a. Up to a half bottle of your favorite wine
   b. One glass of wine if your client is drinking an alcoholic beverage
   c. None; non-alcoholic beverages are always appropriate

7. When eating bread, you will show your impeccable table manners if you:
   a. Cut the bread in half and butter each side before biting from one half

b. Butter one side of the whole bread before taking a bite

c. Cut one small piece at a time and butter it on the plate before eating it

8. You are a woman and have just finished a business luncheon. While seated, you pull a small mirror from your purse and reapply your lipstick for a fresher look. Is this correct?

Yes ___ No ___

9. You had a luncheon meeting with a potential client at their corporate office. Two days later, you fax a typed thank you note to the client. Is this correct?

Yes ___ No ___

10. You are conducting a meeting with a client and some of your staff members. The recommended seating arrangement to facilitate consensus is:

    a. A "U" shaped seating

    b. A round table

    c. A rectangular table

    d. A classroom setup with the head table in front

The following pages will answer these questions. If you want to know the correct answers now, turn to page 199.

THE NEW MALE–FEMALE ETIQUETTE

The golden rule of relationships has been: "Treat others as you would like to be treated." The new platinum rule of this decade is: "Treat others as *they want* to be treated." According to author Letitia Baldrige, today's well-mannered executives follow a double-standard behavior. They treat women as colleagues and team members during the day, but they treat their wives and female friends at home in a different manner. Women have traded the special deference they've received as females for more equality at work. At home, most women want their doors opened and their chairs pulled back. But at the office women want to be treated with respect and as team members. They want to be admired for their skills—not for their looks. With women in executive positions, a new set of manners evolved based on *collegiality*. People are supposed to treat each other according to rules of protocol—not gender. In the business arena, it is not necessary for one gender to come to the aid of the other whenever there is a need for assistance.

In her book *Business Protocol,* Jan Yager says that when she conducted a business etiquette survey with a variety of industries and companies throughout the United States, she found that 77 percent wrote that it is considered proper etiquette at their company for a man to open the door for a woman; 57 percent said it was proper etiquette for a woman to open the door for a man. However, the age-old practice of a man standing up when a woman enters his office seems to be on the way out since a wopping 75 percent wrote that at their company men do not stand up if a woman enters the office. It seems that as women are being treated more equally in the business world, some of the old-fashioned social graces are being omitted from the corporate setting.

Despite these changes, in hospitality, many of the social graces are still valid because when, interacting with guests, many of them may not be a part of the business world; therefore, women guests may expect the same treatment at our properties as they enjoy in social settings.

Having a door opened and a chair pulled out for a woman by a man may still be considered polite in almost all corporate settings. When participants in our etiquette seminars ask about how to deal with these age-old social graces, my suggestion is that when anyone—male or female—initiates a gesture such as opening a door, pulling out a chair, helping with packages or coats, and so forth, it is appropriate to receive and appreciate these courtesies with graciousness.

Rather than our simply following certain rules just because we are dealing with a man or a woman, know that there is an emerging trend that recognizes that courtesy does not have anything to do with gender. Ask yourself: Which role am I playing in this situation? When dealing with coworkers and colleagues inside and out of your workplace, hierarchy is a more appropriate criteria to follow when in doubt. For example, junior managers should assist senior managers with doors, seats and so forth. Women in the office should take care not to mistake sincere politeness from a man for some form of harassment or discrimination.

When interacting with guests, the social graces are still appropriate and welcomed. It is good manners to extend some of the graciousness that men are expected to offer to female guests such as:

- When ascending an escalator with a woman, a man should allow the woman to precede him.
- When descending an escalator with a woman, a man should precede the woman.
- When accompanying a woman on the street, a man should walk on the outside, close to the curb.
- At a luncheon or dinner function with a woman, a man should offer to seat her by holding her chair.
- When a woman excuses herself from the dinner table for a moment, the man who is seated closest to her should acknowledge her departure/return by standing.

In the business arena today, whether you are dealing with peers or colleagues, treating everyone the same is good business etiquette. Whether you are a man or a woman in business today, it is simple courtesy to:

- Move quickly to open a door for anyone walking nearby who has his or her hands full.
- Pick up what someone else has dropped if they cannot retrieve it as easily.
- Open the door for the rest of your group to pass through, if you get to it first.
- Stand to greet a visitor who enters your office.
- Briefly exit a crowded elevator to let other people off even if it is not your destination floor.
- Assist a colleague struggling to get in and out of their coat.
- Extend your hand for introductions.
- Position a client in the curbside back seat when entering a cab.

- Arrange to pay the bill when you are inviting a male or a female for a business luncheon or dinner meeting.

Being attentive to others regardless of gender makes the male-female relationships more pleasant and the work environment more comfortable for everyone.

THE ART OF INTRODUCTIONS

The most important element of introductions even if you forget someone's name is simply *to do* them. People would rather you ask their name than not be introduced. Failing to introduce someone is the same as not recognizing their presence, and this can cause uncomfortable feelings that could damage a business relationship. When you forget a person's name, it is appropriate to ask for their assistance by saying something like: "Please help me to remember your name," rather than neglecting to introduce the person to others. If you need to ask a person's name, make sure you use it again in the conversation as a way to show that you appreciate their help and to assist you remembering their name in the future. When someone is struggling to recall your name, quickly come to their rescue and tell them.

Some people freeze up because they worry too much about the proper procedure. Again, the most important thing is to just do them. The easiest rule to remember is: *Look at and say the name of the most important person* **first.** Depending on the formality of the situation, you will use different expressions. Looking at the most important person and saying their name first shows deference for this person and implies that you are asking permission to give them the gift of a new name with the attached responsibilities. In the business arena, this is the order of the most important person, regardless of gender:

1. Clients
2. Senior executives
3. Junior executives

EXAMPLE, A FORMAL INTRODUCTION:

"Mr. Anderson (your client), *may I introduce* Ms. Brown (your boss), our director of marketing?"

EXAMPLE, A LESS FORMAL INTRODUCTION:

"Mr. Anderson (your client), *I'd like to introduce* Ms. Brown (your boss), our director of marketing."

When using the word *introduce,* avoid using the words *"to you"* or *"you to;"* it may change the order of a person's importance or may get confusing. For example, if you say: "Mr. Anderson (your client), I'd like to introduce *you to* Ms. Brown (your boss), our director of marketing. Now, Ms. Brown became the most important person.

Another simple way to do introductions when the situation is less formal is to use what our seminar participants call *The Magic Formula:* You will still look at and say the name of the most important person first and then use this phrase—*I'd like you to meet...*

EXAMPLE, A LESS FORMAL INTRODUCTION:

"Mr. Anderson (your client), *I'd like you to meet* Ms. Brown (your boss), our director of marketing.

EXAMPLE, A LESS INFORMAL INTRODUCTION:

"Mr. Anderson (your client), *this is* Ms. Brown (your boss), our director of marketing.

When doing introductions, keep them consistent and brief. Offer an equivalent amount of information about each person in turn: first and last names, position, relation to you, relation to the company and any common interest.

When you are at a group business gathering, it is always correct and expected that you walk up to others and introduce yourself. In a dining situation you should introduce yourself to those sitting next to you if you have not been previously introduced. Regardless of gender, in business we should always conduct introductions standing; it is a sign of respect and makes the initiation of a business relationship more equal. In tandem with the introduction, is a genuine smile and a handshake which will express your pleasure in meeting the person. In answering an introduction, a simple reply such as: "I'm glad to meet you" or "How do you do?" will always be appropriate.

YOUR HANDSHAKE

A handshake has a long history of remedying sticky situations. In fact, it was first employed as a way for gentlemen to show each other that they were not armed. Today a handshake is the most accepted possibility of personal touch in business. It is the first step to building a lasting business relationship. Your appearance and your words will be confirmed by the way you shake hands. Others will judge you by your handshake. When hiring managers and sales employees, one of our hotel clients includes the type of handshake of the applicants as one of the criteria in the selection process. A firm handshake conveys confidence, assurance and competence. By the same token, a limp and fish-like handshake may cause others to think that you are weak. A handshake that offers only the front half of the fingers may be interpreted that you do not want to become too involved. Make sure that your grip is firm but not too overpowering; I cannot tell you the times I have had to rescue my small hand from a person with a bone-crusher handshake. Handshaking is not an athletic contest!

A fingers-only handshake may mean lack of involvement.

A double-clasped handshake is considered condescending.

A bone-crusher handshake is overpowering.

A firm handshake conveys confidence and builds lasting business relationships.

Shake hands from the elbow, not from the shoulder. Grasp the other person's hand completely with your palm open. Press your web—the skin between your thumb and index finger—into the other person's web. Hold for about three or four seconds, but not so long that a person feels the need to rescue their hand. In most business situations the double-clasped handshake is considered condescending; it should be saved to express condolence for the loss of a loved one. Check your handshake with a colleague who will give you honest feedback. A firm, confident handshake will enhance your professional image.

Handshakes, of course, can be initiated by either you or the other person; but, it shows confidence when it comes first from you. Reach out and extend your hand to anyone with whom you are doing business—male or female. When do you shake hands? During introductions, to greet clients, vendors, visitors, to say good-by, to congratulate, when you run into someone outside your office and when you leave a gathering attended by people from outside the company.

RISING TO THE OCCASION

The expression of someone rising to the occasion originally was used to describe how confident people will stand when a situation requires their attention. People who stand show that they can take care of whatever business is at hand. In office situations, when a visitor—no matter of what gender—enters a room, the people from the company should stand as a welcoming gesture. In business social activities, women do not remain seated when other business people enter a room. Women should rise as readily to their feet as any man to show the visitor respect. When a senior manager enters your office, you should stand as a sign of deference. If a person of a higher rank enters your office several times during a day, you do not have to stand every time; a smile and eye contact is enough to acknowledge their presence.

Always rise to shake hands with others for introductions or for greetings. When you remain seated, the person standing is in a more dominant and powerful position. Before I start a presentation or a seminar, I go around the room to meet as many people as I can. To my surprise, some participants, male and female, remain seated when we shake hands. Standing is the most assertive way to begin and sometimes to conduct a business encounter. When you stand you show respect, you feel energized and you can let others know that a meeting or a conversation is ending.

SEATED, PLEASE!

When attending a meeting in a restaurant or an executive's office, junior managers should wait until senior managers signal to them where to sit. If you are the senior manager or the chairman of the meeting, you should indicate the proper place for the participants to sit. It is very uncomfortable for people to stand in a room and wonder where to sit.

You may recall that King Arthur sat his knights at a round table following wizard Merlin's advice. Merlin suggested that this seating would minimize conflict. This principle is still valid today. If you want to get consensus and agreement at a meeting, a round table will facilitate this process. When you position chairs in a circle, you encourage relatively equal contributions from all group members. Rectangular tables define rank positions. The head of the table is saved for the "power person"—the most senior person in rank. At a rectangular table the two short ends will be the most powerful positions. (When the table is too long, though, the most important seat is the end at which the "power person" sits.) The other important positions are those to the right and the left of the power person. When meetings are conducted in a horseshoe or U shape, the focus of attention would be at the "head of the table." If chairs are placed side by side in theater or classroom style, participants get the message that they are there "to listen not to talk." Savvy executives today who want to empower team members and promote effective teamwork are conducting meetings at round tables, instead of the traditional rectangular, with great success.

When given a choice of seating at a meeting whether conducted in an office, conference room or dining room, here are some tips:

- Choose a chair over a couch. A chair gives you a more powerful position than the lower couch seating.
- If you must sit in a couch, sit at the edge and avoid the temptation of slouching and losing your confident posture.
- Sit next to a person with whom you want to avoid a direct interchange. Sitting across from that person forces communication since you will need to keep eye contact.
- Sit as close to the leader as protocol permits.
- Women benefit from not crossing their legs. Crossing your legs stops circulation and makes you look uptight. Besides, it is not the most comfortable or business-like position when wearing a skirt that rises above the knee. Instead, cross your legs at the ankles.
- Watch your posture while sitting. Sitting erectly gives you more confidence and control of the conversation than when you are slouching.

SMOKING

Smoking is becoming less and less acceptable in the United States. With the emphasis on public health, many companies are banning smoking completely from their offices and facilities. Smoking is no longer appropriate in business settings. Guests and employees are requesting more smoke-free environments. John

Hallowell, a hotel executive, says that in his properties the majority of the guests prefer non-smoking rooms and the number is ever increasing. Some properties have designated smoking areas for employees and for guests. Therefore, if you still want to light a cigarette, use either open or specially designated areas.

In hospitality, however, we interact with clients and guests from other cultures in which smoking is still accepted. Even though meeting planners tell us that foreign visitors are more and more aware of the growing American non-smoking policy, some European and Japanese businesspersons would find it rude to be asked not to smoke. Offering private dining or meeting rooms for your smoking guests is an appropriate way to accommodate their needs.

TELEPHONE ETIQUETTE

The telephone is your link to the outside world. Through the telephone we give and receive information, pass instructions to people and establish and strengthen business relationships. Much business is initiated and much is lost over the telephone. Good manners and professionalism over the telephone are as important as in face-to-face contact. In hospitality, many times the first encounter with a client is over the telephone, so your telephone skills give a positive or a negative first impression.

People form impressions about you by the way you speak to them on the telephone. Even though others cannot see your facial expressions or your overall physical appearance, they do form a mental picture of you based on words, tone and voice quality. Also your mood comes through the phone. Some people keep a mirror next to their phone to be sure they smile when answering the phone.

A pleasant phone voice takes practice. You can check your voice by recording yourself and asking a friend for an honest feedback. Breathing, pausing and speaking from your stomach—not from your throat—will help you to project a well-modulated and pleasant voice.

Here are some basic tools for your telephone etiquette:

- Remember that when you place a call, you are doing it because this is a convenient time for you. It may or may not be a good time for the person you are calling. Asking the person you are calling: "Is this a convenient time to talk?" is a very appropriate way to begin a phone encounter. If the person says no, ask when would be a convenient time for you to call back. Do not force a call on someone; you will not get the results and/or you can damage the relationship.

- When you place a call, listen carefully to the other person's tone of voice—you may even want to close your eyes—and mimic or *"mirror" the voice.* This will build an immediate rapport. If you call someone who answers with a low voice and you begin the encounter with a high enthusiastic voice, it is very difficult to get the conversation to what Sharon Drew Morgan in her book *Sales on the Line* calls the *"we space."* Once there is that initial trust, you go back to your normal voice tone and pitch to continue the conversation.

- Write down the key points you want to discuss. It is a pleasure talking with someone who says: "There are three things I'd like to talk to you about." It gives structure to the conversation and helps both parties stay focused.

- Identify yourself by giving your name, your company—or department if it's an internal call—and the purpose of your call. One of my clients has a sticker on his phone that says "The reason I'm calling is..."

- If you are an unknown caller and a secretary answers the phone for the person you want to reach, it is appropriate to identify yourself by name, your company and the purpose of your call. It is rude to pose as a personal friend just to get your call through.

- If you need to leave a message with a secretary, leave your name, company, phone number and a convenient time for the person to return your call. This will help avoid telephone tag.

- If you have to put a person on hold, please ask for permission. *"May I put you on hold for a few minutes?"* If it is taking more than a few minutes, go back to the person and ask if she/he wants to keep holding or if they would prefer that you call back. Remember that the first person you are speaking with has priority. You should tell the second caller that you are on another line and you will call back. When you return to the person on hold always say: *"Thank you for holding."*

- When conducting a meeting in your office, put your calls on hold through a secretary, through voice mail or ask someone to answer the calls for you. It is rude to chat over the phone with someone else when you are having a meeting with a visitor. One of my hotel clients explained at the beginning of our meeting that he was waiting for a very important international call he would need to take. He even gave me some material to read while he took this call. This was an example of etiquette and class.

- One of the most important things to do with your phone calls is to *return them as soon as possible or at least within 24 hours.* If the person is not available when you return the call, to avoid telephone tag leave alternative times when your can be reached.

- Answer your phone yourself if possible and answer it before three rings. The general manager of one of our hotel clients answers his own phone. When I asked him about it, he said: "If I'm available to answer calls, better me than someone else. It saves time to both parties." I was impressed!

- When answering the phone include the four key elements of:
    1. A greeting
    2. Name of company (or department for internal calls)
    3. Your name
    4. Offer for assistance

EXAMPLE, EXTERNAL CALL:
"Good morning! _____ restaurant, this is Lawrence Parker. How may I help you?"

INTERNAL CALL
"Good evening! Catering Department, Sheila speaking. How may I help you?"

• When you answer a phone for a colleague, identify yourself and your colleague's office:
"Good afternoon! Jim Martin's office, George Anderson speaking. How may I help you?"

Take a complete message including name, company, phone number, purpose of call if necessary and the best time to return the call. Your colleague will appreciate this type of assistance.

• When callers do not identify themselves, it is rude to ask: *"Who is this?"* Instead you may ask: *"To whom am I speaking?"* or *"Whom shall I say is calling?"* or *"May I say who is calling?"*
• When answering a phone for someone avoid explanations such as:

AVOID	USE INSTEAD
He/she isn't here yet	He/she's not in his/her office at the moment
He/she is on her break	He/she is away from his/her desk at the moment
He/she is at lunch	He/she is not available at the moment
He/she left early today	He/she is out of the office until tomorrow
He/she is on vacation	He/she will be out of the office for the next two weeks
He/she is sick today	He/she is not in the office today

And of course, *never* say:
"I believe he/she went to the men's/lady's room."
"He/she has a doctor's appointment this afternoon."
"He/she's at the beauty/barber shop."

Avoid sentences that have *lost* customers:
1. "I can't put your call through unless I can say who's calling."
2. "I don't have anything to do with your problem."
3. "She/he's busy—would you call back?"

4. "There is nothing I can do about it; it's company policy."
5. "I just came in; could you call back in about 10 to 15 minutes?"
6. "We are ready to close; would you call back in the morning?"

- If you get disconnected during a call, the person who initiated the call is responsible for calling back, unless you are speaking with a client. It is a courtesy for you to call back a client regardless of who initiated the call.
- When you finish a conversation, end graciously. For example: "I'm glad you called" or "Thanks for calling."
- Let the caller hang up first before you ring off.

High Tech Etiquette

New technology has created new applications for manners in the workplace. Voice mail and other computer communications require you to be just as courteous as you should be in person, on the telephone and in written communication. Here are some guidelines for high-tech courtesy:

Voice Mail-Speaker Phones

Voice mail has become a common way to answer phone calls when employees cannot take calls personally. When recording your greeting, leave a short message. A message that begins: "I can't come to the phone right now because I'm out of the office" is a waste of a caller's time. Think about it! Obviously you are not available for one reason or another; if your were, you would take the call. A simpler message could be: "Hello! This is Robert Kramer. Please leave me a message so I can call you back. Thank you for calling!" or "Hello! This is Robert Kramer. Your call is important to me, so please leave me your message and I'll call you back. Have a nice day!"

If you are out of your office frequently and you want to leave a personalized message with detailed information, you could begin with something like: "This is Louise Reed. I'm in a meeting on

Monday from 9:00 to noon…" If you give another number they can dial, be sure it's not another mail box. Leave instructions for the person who will take your calls during that time.

Office equipment such as answering machines and speaker phones create opportunities to violate confidentiality and privacy. One of our seminar participants shared an embarrassing experience: "A salesperson called the company vice president's office with information related to the business and asked if this was a good time for the vice president to talk. The caller didn't know that the vice president was on the speaker phone in the middle of a meeting." If you need to use your speaker phone to free your hands for other tasks, ask the other person's permission. Say something like: "May I use the speaker phone so I can go through these papers while we discuss it?"

It's not professional to leave an intimate message on voice mail— you never know who's listening. Limit the use of voice mail to business. When leaving a message on voice mail, make notes of the key points of your message before calling. If you are not prepared when the machine answers, hang up, get ready and call back. Speak clearly and more slowly than if you were talking face-to-face. When leaving a phone number, say the number twice. If you want the call returned, give a time when you are most reachable.

Cellular Phones

Many cellular phones are being used incorrectly. Whenever you make or receive a call from a car phone, identify yourself first, using both your name and your company's name and explain that you are using a car phone. There are a few occasions in which it is appropriate to call from a car phone: when you are late for an appointment, you need directions, you got lost or you must give someone urgent information. Be brief and make an appointment to call again from your office when you can devote all your attention to the phone call. It is impolite to initiate or to conduct a sales call from a car phone.

The number one business blunder with cellular phones is using them in inappropriate places such as on the golf course or at the movies or a restaurant; in fact, never make or receive a call at a table in a restaurant, unless it's an emergency.

Many professionals in hospitality wear pagers. If you do not want to be paged, don't wear your pager. In a public place or during an important meeting, turn off the beeper sound so the pager only vibrates if someone needs to page you. Then, excuse yourself and make the necessary phone call.

FAX MACHINES

Using the fax machine also requires some common sense and courtesy: Fax only information that must be transmitted to the other party faster than regular mail. Offer the other person a choice to send the information by mail or fax. Do not assume that everyone prefers faxed information. It is recommended that you send the hard copy after you send the fax for communications with clients and vendors. Remember that the fax is not a personal way to communicate with someone since it's possible that many people will read your message. Personal faxing can hurt your image and the image of your company; therefore, do not send jokes, cartoons, opinions of people, programs or confidential information. Also avoid sending a 30-page brochure or program via fax. Thirty pages is time-consuming and costly.

Sending a thank you, congratulation or condolence note by fax is inappropriate. Only a handwritten note is appropriate in these situations. If your handwriting is not very clear, you may type it. Use a heavy-weight stationery with your name or the name of your company on it. A handwritten note says that you care about this business relationship and you have taken the time and effort to make this communication special. In these times of "high-tech/low touch," these personal efforts mean a great deal to people. When we go through our piles of correspondence, we can identify the handwritten notes, and we know they are something special. Taking the time and effort to write personal notes will do wonders for your clients, your colleagues and for your career. Remember to send a thank you note within 24 to 48 hours after the event.

How you look and sound over a technical device or in writing is as important as how you look and sound in person.

DINING ETIQUETTE

"The world was my oyster, but I used the wrong fork," said Oscar Wilde 90-odd years ago. Today, using the wrong fork can be hazardous to your career. When we interviewed top executives in the hospitality industry for this book, they said that it is critical that their employees have as much social polish at the dinner table as they do in the meeting room. Poor table manners, they said, is an embarrassment to the company and damages the company's image. Entertaining clients is an essential part of the hospitality business. When they have to choose between candidates for a position, many of them conduct interviews during meals to observe if the candidate's table manners match their resume qualifications.

Mastering impeccable table manners gives you the confidence to concentrate on your guests, clients or colleagues. You want to focus on the conversation instead of worrying about which fork to use. Understanding the flow of the different courses in a meal and handling them with ease and good manners is as important as other technical skills. Think of a dining experience as a symphony orchestra in which each piece of silverware has a function and, along with the food and people, contributes to a smooth experience that enhances a business relationship.

PLACE SETTINGS

The silver and flatware laid out in this drawing is one of the most common place settings for a four-course, semi-formal meal. Note that the napkin could be placed to the left or in the center of the dinner plate.

The simple way to determine which utensil to use is to work from the outside in. For example, on the left side of the plate, you move inward from the salad fork to the entrée fork. A very small fork such as for seafood could be on the far right or left. There will never be more than three utensils on each side of the plate. This is why the dessert fork and spoon are usually placed above the dinner plate. Don't touch them until desert is served. Then, you will move them to the side of the dessert plate keeping them as they were initially placed—the fork to the left and the spoon to the right. If the desert only requires a fork, the spoon is used for coffee.

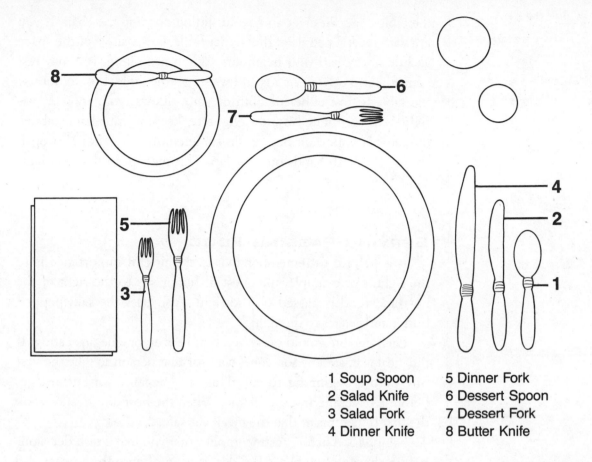

1 Soup Spoon	5 Dinner Fork
2 Salad Knife	6 Dessert Spoon
3 Salad Fork	7 Dessert Fork
4 Dinner Knife	8 Butter Knife

It often happens at a function that we wonder whose salad, roll plate or wine glass belongs to whom. My colleague Mary Jane Barnes says an easy way to remember which ones are yours is to always look for: *"Liquids on your right, solids on your left."* This way, you can take the glasses located on the right side of your plate and the salad and bread plates located on your left. If the person seated to your left doesn't realize that they just placed their roll on your bread and butter plate, thank the person for the roll and begin to eat it.

SEATING

When you are the host or hostess, you should extend the "power seat" to your client. Seat yourself with your back facing the door or the main part of the room. Sit with your chair several inches from the table edge. Sit erect and avoid sliding down in the chair. If you are with several people at the dinner table, be sensitive of the space and do not crowd your neighbors. When not eating, you may rest your forearm or your hands and wrists on the table, but do not use the table to rest either or both of your elbows (your mother was right!). In corporate business etiquette, keeping your hands above the table is important because in some cultures it is not appropriate to have both hands on your lap. This may mean that you have something to hide.

SERVING-PASSING FOOD

It is helpful to remember that everything of importance is to the right. For example, the guest of honor sits to the right of the host and food is passed on the right. Also pass the salt, pepper, butter and sauces to the right.

Each person should be served before everyone begins eating. If the meal is hosted by someone, wait for that person to take the first bite before beginning to eat. This rule began a long time ago, before refrigeration was available. When the host and hostess took the first bite it meant that the meal was safe.

Salting food before tasting implies that you make rash decisions before checking the facts! Besides, it is an offense to the chef and implies that the food was not properly seasoned. Henry Ford and J.C.Penney built their management staff on this premise. Can you imagine how many candidates they must have taken to lunch?

TALKING BUSINESS

If the purpose of your meeting is business, it is not appropriate to leap into the topic as soon as you are seated. Take your time and allow your guest to relax. Begin with small talk. It is important to establish or to reinforce rapport with your guest.

Do not bring up business before the entree is consumed. Be sensitive to when your guest is ready to talk business. Most people prefer to wait and talk business only over dessert and coffee. Others may want to plunge right in; therefore, begin discussing business when the client appears ready. A pleasant conversation and meal will often do more for your business relations than a "nuts and bolts" discussion. Be especially sensitive when entertaining clients from other cultures. Americans in general tend to rush over meals. For most cultures, dining is a ritual that flows slowly and pleasantly. Do not be surprised if your client does not even discuss any business over a meal. Your guest will give you signals, so be alert.

At a business meal, don't place your briefcase, handbag or stack of files on the table. Put them on the floor out of the way of your server and other traffic. When it is time to discuss business, wait until the table has been cleared of only coffee and tea and then put a few papers at a time on the table.

At a cocktail party or trade show function, circulating among as many people as possible can be a business builder. Do not treat this function as a mini-dinner; use this opportunity to meet and network with new people or to strengthen relationships with your existing clients. At a cocktail event, hold your drink in your left hand so you free your right for shaking hands. When joining a group, get into the conversation by asking questions. Try to make the other person talk more than you do; questioning is a good way to do this.

NAPKIN

After you are seated, wait to see if the waiter will unfold your napkin for you. If he does not, unfold it and place it on your lap. If you need to leave the table during a meal, place the napkin on your chair, not on the table. A napkin on the chair tells the waiter that you will come back. When you finish your meal, place your napkin loosely folded on the right side of the table. This indicates that you are ready to leave.

BREAD

Select your bread and put it on your bread plate. Break a small piece off of the roll and leave the remainder on the plate until you are ready to eat another piece. Butter the small piece on the plate and eat it. Do not butter the whole roll or cut it in two like sandwich bread. And, of course, it is poor manners to bite half of your roll. Food critics say that you can spot a good restaurant by the quality of the bread. You can also measure a person's table manners by the way they eat their bread.

DRINKING

Today's society is very health conscious. In business it has become almost a norm not to drink alcoholic beverages at a luncheon meeting. Those people who refuse an alcoholic beverage, even if everyone else orders one, are no longer considered teetotalers. Whether you are a guest or a host, remember that drinking mars decision-making abilities. When your guest orders a non-alcoholic beverage, the proper etiquette is for you to order something similar; ordering wine or hard liquor is inappropriate. If you only want a club soda or iced tea, let your guest know that while you may not care for a drink, it's perfectly all right with you if he or she does. If you sense that it would be proper to accompany your guest, one glass of wine is the most you are supposed to drink at a luncheon meeting.

At private functions where wine is served, if you decide not to drink any alcohol, you may want to let the wait person pour your wine and, then, not drink it or just take one or two sips. This is the most effective way to avoid having the efficient staff continue to offer wine. Do not put your hand on top of your glass to signal that you do not want any wine, do not turn your glass upside-down and avoid saying that you do not drink. (These actions will only bring attention to your non-drinking status and cause additional work for the wait staff; it is almost impossible for a server attending many guests to remember that you do not desire wine.)

While entertaining clients at other functions other than luncheon meetings, such as cocktail parties, barbecues, dinners and banquets, where savoring excellent wines and other alcoholic beverages is an essential part of the entertaining in hospitality, *discretion* is your best policy. You must know your limits. Select the type and amount of alcoholic beverages that is healthy for you. You want to be sure that your system can handle the alcohol you choose without losing your demeanor or your control. Regardless of the setting, you are always representing your company. Keeping your professionalism at the dinner table and at the bar is as important as it is in the meeting room.

SMOKING AT THE TABLE

As mentioned before, it is an established medical fact that smoking is a health hazard. Smoking is less tolerated in public places in the United States. However, there are still some of your customers, colleagues or providers that may still want to smoke at the table. With restaurants now having designated sections for smoking, it makes it easy for you as a host/ess to know your client's preference.

At private affairs, if smoke really affects your health, it is appropriate to ask to be seated at a table where people do not smoke. In situations where this is not possible (and when you are not the host or hostess), if a smoker at your table lights up, try to voice your objection in a gentle way, depersonalizing your request. For example: "I'm sorry, but I'm allergic to smoke. Would you mind smoking on the terrace?" Or, "I'm sorry, I'm allergic to smoke; would you mind terribly waiting to smoke until later?" This places the blame on a medical problem, not on the smoker's habit. *If the smoker is the host or hostess, a client or the guest of honor, it is recommended just to let them smoke without such comments or restrictions.* This is especially important when entertaining foreign clients for whom smoking is still acceptable.

In any case, smoking should never be done while there is food on the table. Do not light up at the table until after everyone has finished dessert. And, of course, if you smoke, be careful to exhale away from people's faces; it might require shifting your position in your seat to be able to control the stream.

In today's business world, it is an asset to be a non-smoker— not only for your health, but for the ability to interact with others easily without the burden of an additional issue that may cause discomfort to those with whom we work, entertain and serve.

ORDERING FOOD

If you are hosting the meal, recommend a few dishes to your guest. Your recommendation clues the guest to the price range that you are planning for the meal. If you are dining at your company's restaurant, this is a golden opportunity for you to display the excellent cuisine that your chefs offer; recommend a few of the specialties to your guest. When choosing your own meal, stay away from slippery pastas, bony fish and fowl and cheese-topped soups. Be careful with food that is difficult to eat, such as olives, peas, artichokes. Cherry tomatoes are another example of foods to avoid; they tend to squirt on your guest's clothes. (Regard them as decoration only; one of my chef friends says he only serves them when he's having a bad day!) Choose simple foods such as chicken and fish fillet. Do not order anything that will distract you from the conversation or that puts you in an awkward position.

To let your guest know that it is all right to order an appetizer or dessert, you may want to make some recommendations or order one for yourself. When the food is served buffet style, show the buffet to your guest explaining the options available, and then let your guest proceed to the line first. When you take your own food, take only as much as you will eat. Avoid piling large amounts of food on your plate; you can always go back for seconds.

SOUP

Soup or bouillon served in a handled cup or even small bowl (oriental fashion) may be drunk instead of being spooned. If there are dumplings or shredded mushrooms, vegetables or other garnish floating on top, they should be eaten first with the spoon, before the liquid part of the soup is drunk. When eating thick soup, it is appropriate to eat the solid portion—such as vegetables—from the end of the spoon. Otherwise, all soups are eaten by sipping from the side of the spoon. Spoon your soup away from you toward the center of the bowl. The spoon should rest where it is least likely to fall. When resting the soup spoon, place it either in the bowl or on the plate upon which the soup sits. If a cup is used, place the spoon on the plate, if a soup plate is used; if not, leave it

1. Hold the soup spoon in the right hand with the thumb on top.

2. Spoon soup away from you toward the center of the bowl and not toward you. Sip the soup from the side of the spoon.

resting in the soup container. Tip the bowl away from you when spooning the last bit of soup. And need we add, never "slurp" your soup!

EATING STYLES

There are two basic styles of holding flatware while dining:

The *American* style is called "Zig-Zag." The fork is held in the left hand, tines down; the knife in the right hand as shown in the drawing. You use the fork to hold the food while cutting a bite-size piece with the knife. It is never appropriate to cut more than one bite-size piece at a time. After cutting one piece of food, lay the knife across the top of the plate with the serrated edge toward you, transferring the fork to your opposite hand and finally inserting the piece of food in your mouth. The entire process is repeated as your need to cut food continues. When not cutting, the knife remains resting across the upper right quarter of the plate with the blade toward the center while eating proceeds using the fork alone. When you are resting, your knife stays at the one o'clock position with blade turned inward and your fork at the four o'clock position with tines up.

To indicate that you have finished eating, the utensils are placed together on the plate with the fork tines up and the knife

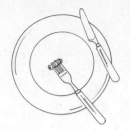

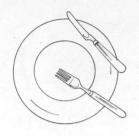

1. *Cutting food.*

2. *Eating the food with fork/knife in right position.*

3. *Resting position.*

4. *"I'm finished" position.*

turned inward in the lower, right-hand portion of the plate between the clock positions of four and six. This assures that they will not slide off as the plate is being removed. The "I'm finished position" signals to the wait staff that they can remove your plate and utensils. The position of the knife tells the server whether you are still eating or you are finished with your meal— one o'clock signals that you are still eating and four to six o'clock signals that you are finished.

The *Continental* style of dining differs from the American style in the following way: Begin with the knife in the right hand and the fork in the left with tines down as shown. To cut bite-size pieces of food, hold the food with the fork and cut with the knife. Then spear the food with the fork—which is still in your left hand—and put it in your mouth. As you continue eating, use the knife as a backstop to assist in spearing the food with the fork. Remember that in the Continental style, using a fork by itself is rarely correct. Once the knife and fork are used together during a single course, they must be used together throughout the entire course. Occasionally, some courses do not require the use of a knife. In those instances your place setting will not have one. The fork is used as in the American style—placed in the right hand with the tines pointed up. When resting between bites, the knife and fork are crossed on the plate with the fork over the knife with the prongs pointed down in an inverted V. The well-informed wait staff will never remove your plate with the knife and fork crossed because they know that you are not finished with your meal.

When you have completed your main course, the utensils are placed together on the plate with the fork tines down and the knife turned inward anywhere between the clock positions of four and six. This position of your silverware indicates that you have finished eating. The "I'm finished" position in the Continental style is similar to the one used in the American style; the difference is that in the Continental style, the fork is placed with tines down and in the American style, the fork is placed with tines up. Both send a clear signal to the wait staff that they can remove your plate and silverware.

CONTINENTAL STYLE

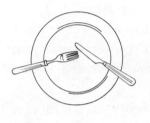 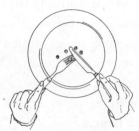  

1. Holding the utensils.　　　*2. Cutting the food.*　　　*3. Resting position.*　　　*4. "I'm finished" position.*

EATING DESSERT

When the main course is finished, bring the utensils that are placed on top of the dinner plate to the sides of the plate: the fork to the left and the spoon to the right. Dessert that includes solids and creamy or liquid food may be eaten with the fork in the left hand, prongs down, and the spoon in the right. Eat with the spoon. The fork can serve as a pusher. If it is cake or pie you may use only the fork. For ice cream or pudding, use only the spoon. Leave the other utensil in place on the table. To indicate that you are finished with your dessert, place both utensils together at either side on your plate.

Many professionals today are switching to the Continental style of dining because it is more accepted internationally and easier to employ. It will be necessary to practice the method in your own home until you become comfortable enough to use it in public.

Whether you are using the American or the Continental style of dining, here are some do's and don'ts of table manners:

- Do not hold utensils in your hand if you are not using them.
- Never gesture with utensils in your hand.
- Always put your utensils in the resting position between bites; don't let them be all over your plate.
- Don't talk with your mouth full. Take small bites so you can talk easily at any time after you swallow small portions of food.
- Do not blow your nose or sneeze at the table. If a sneezing attack occurs, turn away from your companion and do not use your napkin. Take a restroom break if you must.
- Do not remove inedible foods or bones to a napkin. Instead, discreetly bring a fork or a spoon to your lips—use your other hand as a "cover tent"— and deposit the item onto it and lower it to your plate.
- If food requires a knife, spoon or fork, you must not eat it or touch it with your fingers.
- It is impolite to inspect and freshen makeup at the dinner table. Personal tasks like powdering your nose and brushing your hair should take place in the restroom. Some etiquette consultants—to my amusement—suggest that you can reapply lipstick at the dinner table. In this case, the "no gender" rule applies: How would it look if a man took out his small shaver and shaved after the meal was finished? Any grooming activities should be conducted in the restroom or in the privacy of your office.
- Try not to finish every last morsel of food on your plate, and try to keep pace with others with whom you are dining. Remember that the focus of business dining is on the get-together, not on the eating.

PAYING THE BILL

In hospitality many of the dining meetings are conducted at the property's restaurants. This makes it easier to deal with the issue of who pays the bill. Regardless of gender, whoever initiates the meeting or whoever is in a senior capacity should pick up the tab. Some men still feel uncomfortable when a woman pays for a meal. To avoid this awkward situation if you are a woman, give your credit card in advance to the maitre'd; he will have the check and card returned to you on a plate. If all your plans go awry and the bill is presented to your male companion, ask him to pass it on to you. Don't say: "It's mine" or "I'm paying for it." If he objects, tell him: "Our company is delighted to take you out." By letting him know that this is the company's treat, you should curtail his reluctance.

Any business meeting that involves food—whether it is a breakfast, lunch, cocktail party or dinner—demands impeccable table manners. Remember that you are there for business first, not to eat. Stick to familiar foods and eat slowly since that is polite; it also indicates that you are confident, reserved and in control of yourself and your food. If you are not sure of what to do with any utensil or food, observe and follow the leaders. The pleasure and the goal of business dining is to ease and facilitate working relationships. Let your perfect table manners reinforce your professional image of excellence.

THE ART OF
SELECTING UNIFORMS

otel, motel, resort and restaurant developers spend time, energy and large sums of money deciding on the interior and exterior design and decoration of their properties. The physical appearance of a property conveys the type of establishment it is and the type of service it provides. Selecting the uniforms of the employees that work there is just as important as selecting the decor. After all, the front line staff create the first and most lasting impressions with customers and guests; therefore, their appearance and grooming is critical to achieving that *first* best impression.

As important as the task of selecting uniforms is, it often becomes a nightmare for managers who have enough difficulty choosing their own clothes. They are assigned the duty of making choices in an area in which they do not have the skills or enough information. It's not an impossible task, though, and there are considerations to keep in mind before even looking through a uniform catalog. First, understand that employees who wear a uniform are giving up a prime means of self-expression—choosing how to present themselves to the rest of the world, at least at work. While it is true that a comfortable and attractive uniform will not necessarily make your employees happy, it's also true that an uncomfortable and unattractive one *will* make your employees unhappy and this unhappiness will be reflected in their performance.

Organizations have the responsibility of providing uniforms that are not only attractive to their employees, but are also comfortable and leave some room for individuality. An article published by the *Washington Post* in 1993 referred to some of the employees of a chain store: "The youth upon whom business depend to man their registers are rebelling against jobs that require a crummy uniform along with a hard day's work." And when the CEO of a large, fast food chain wanted to update the corporation's uniforms, he gave his executives the choice of either creating more dignified clothing for their employees or wearing the old uniforms themselves. The uniforms were promptly redesigned.

When I was consulting for a resort property in Virginia, the company decided to redo the bell-staff uniforms. The bellmen had been wearing the same brown and beige, 100 percent polyester uniforms for more than ten years. When asked for their opinion, they complained about how unattractive, uncomfortable and hot they felt in their uniform, especially during the summer. We selected a navy-gray combination of pants, vest and jacket in a wool polyester blend, a light blue shirt and striped tie. Before making the final decision, we asked employees for their feedback. They liked it. Six months later when I went back to the resort, the bellmen sported a new attitude along with their new look. They reported that not only did they feel better about their uniforms, but they were also getting "bigger tips."

On the other hand, most uniforms that hospitality properties provide to their employees are better quality clothes than the ones employees would wear if they had to purchase their own. In addition, the employee saves money since the company purchases the uniforms. A uniform also provides a consistent and appropriate look at all times.

THE RIGHT UNIFORM

The correct uniform is the one that:

- Blends with the style and overall theme of the property;
- Reflects the level of formality of the establishment;

- Is appropriate for the specific job;
- Is comfortable to wear (fabric and fit);
- Is attractive and flattering to the employees (color and style);
- Is easy to accessorize;
- Is easy to care for.

The style, decor and "theme" of the property dictate the general style of the uniforms. At a city hotel, the uniforms would mirror the level of formality of the property, and the rule of thumb is the higher the price of a room, the dressier the uniforms. By the same token, it would be inappropriate to have a formal suit uniform for the front desk employees of a resort property in Arizona. A motel on an interstate highway or a property in a small town may find that, for male employees, sport coats and coordinated trousers, or even a non-traditional dress shirt and trousers, are the appropriate choice to project friendliness and comfort to their traveler customers.

Uniforms must also blend with the decor of the room where the employees will be working. Wall, furniture and carpet colors, fabrics, textures and designs must be considered when selecting the uniforms. You may want to conduct part of the selection process in the room where the employees will be wearing the uniforms. Have the employees try on the samples and ask them to walk around the room or work location to see how well the proposed uniform blends in with the work area. Ask them to perform the movements they normally do in their job to check comfort and flexibility. Taking the time to go through these exercises when selecting uniforms will eliminate costly mistakes which, all too often, have been made when selection was confined to the manager's office.

When deciding on how formal you want your uniforms to be, think of the ways your guests dress when they visit the different areas and services at the property. Of course, there can be different levels of formality at the same property. For example, the uniforms for the employees at the health club will be casual and appealing to the health-conscious guest, and the uniforms of the wait-staff and host/ess at the formal restaurant will be formal.

In the '90s, with the downsizing and flattening of organizations, management strategies are focused on empowering employees; as a result, some of the power symbols are disappearing. This trend has affected the way companies select and purchase uniforms. In this decade, there is less and less emphasis in differentiating employees by the uniforms they wear. Employees are empowered to assist a client whenever there is a need, regardless of their job description.

Large companies are now using the same uniforms for housekeeping and conference employees; wait-staff and bartenders wear the same attire; reservations, front desk and PBX employees wear the same suit. This sharing of uniform styles allows for the mobility of employees to different positions according to the workload in a given department. In addition, when a "behind the scenes" employee comes out to serve a client, wearing the same uniform assures the client of consistent service, regardless of the hierarchy of the employee attending their needs. It is also common that some employees may be doing two or more jobs within the same department, so the same or very similar uniform allows the employees to better attend to guests.

Many restaurant owners who are using exactly the same uniform for captains, wait-staff and runners believe that customers, when seeing a sea of service people around them, feel confident and well taken care of. They reason that a customer doesn't need to know the hierarchy of who is who; the staff already knows who they are and they don't need a different uniform to tell them apart.

Another advantage of having the same uniforms for different positions is financial. It is easier and more cost effective to keep inventory of fewer uniform types.

When selecting uniforms, it is important to consider the level of responsibility of the employee. When assisting one resort property in uniform selection, we debated whether to give the front desk manager a uniform with or without a jacket, so we asked ourselves: If a guest has a serious problem that requires the intervention of a manager, will the employee look more credible in a jacketed uniform? Or, put another way, would a jacket send a message to the guest that says: "I have the authority to make a decision to solve your problem." One of the difficulties that employees face sometimes when trying to solve a client's problem is that the guest is better dressed than they are, so their credibility is diminished. A

1

2

3

4

5

jacket is a symbol of authority and assures the client that the employee can solve their problems. Even in resort properties where the uniforms are more casual, selecting jackets for some positions is important. The use of colorful jackets will send a clear message of credibility, while keeping the resort look of the establishment.

Let's now examine the elements that are used in selecting uniforms: fabric, color, style and accessories. These same elements also work as symbols that send messages of duty, responsibility and hierarchy.

FABRICS: The texture of the fabric chosen contributes to the level of formality: Fine, shiny fabrics such as silk and satin are dressy; a matte finish like cotton is less dressy; and nubby fabrics such as twill and knits are casual.

Dressy fabrics: wool, wool blends, shiny fabric, silk, silk-like, tone-on-tone shirts, tapestry, jacquard, velvet, crepe, faille, broadcloth, chiffon.

Less dressy: linen, cotton, knits, lycra, matte finish, oxford, tweeds, challis, rayon, medium to small prints, geometric, abstract.

Casual: cotton, knits, denim, twill, bold prints for women's blouses or skirts, plaids, madras, corduroy, tweed, florals, realistic, animal, abstract and large geometric prints, checks, tattersall and plaid shirts for men.

COLOR: Color is one of the clothing elements to which the human eye responds first. Color creates invisible waves like music does; soft, light colors evoke feelings of calmness and cleanliness; dark colors give a sense of drama and formality; and medium to light toned neutrals and bright colors are upbeat and casual.

Dressy: black, black and white combinations, solid white for certain uniforms; dark colors such as gray, navy, burgundy, teal, dark green, purple, rust, blue red; light colors in a dressy fabric could include cream, peach, light aqua, light periwinkle and the metalics gold and silver. Note: White is a dressy color in formal settings and especially at a resort.

1

2

3

4

5

6

7

8

LESS DRESSY

1

4

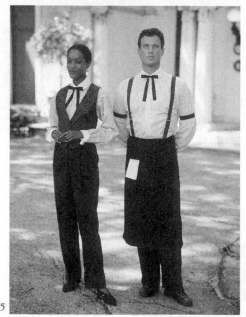

2

5

3

6

Less dressy: medium gray, blue green, raspberry, plum, orange red, royal blue, mauve, turquoise, taupe, beige, fuchsia.

Casual: soft white, beige, khaki, brown, coral, pink, peach, lime green, periwinkle, orange, bright pinks, yellow, light shades, pastels and bright colors

STYLES: The silhouette and design of a garment affect its formality. Straight shoulders and constructed design of a double breasted jacket make it dressier. A gathered cotton long skirt or a polo shirt with an unconstructed design are more casual.

Dressy
    tuxedo
    suits for men
    double-breasted suits for men
    dinner jackets for men
    matching suits for women
    jackets for women
    long skirts
    pant suits for women
    dressy vests for men and women
    ornate trims and braids
    gold and silver silk trims

Less Dressy
    blazer and sport coats for men
    sweater vest or pullover with jacket for men
    colored shirts for men
    striped shirts for men
    button-down shirts
    bolder colors and patterns in ties
    unmatched suits for women
    sweater jackets for women
    printed dresses for women
    skirt and blouse for women
    slacks and blouse for women

Casual
    pants and polo or T-shirts for men and women
    shorts for men and women
    skirt and casual blouse for women

1

2

4

3

5

6

7

ACCESSORIES

Dressy

    pearls for women

    gold or silver shiny necklaces and pins for women

    clear stone earrings, necklace and pins for women

    silk scarves

    silk ties for men (smaller patterns are dressier)

    bold abstract or medallion ties for men

    silk bow ties for men and women

    pocket square for men

    cuff links for men and women

    leather classic belts for men and women

    patent leather belts for women

    higher heel shoes for women

    lace-up shoes for men

Less Dressy

    matte finish accessories for women

    chain necklaces

    matte finish ties for men

    matte finish bow ties for men and women

    club ties for men

    tassel loafers for men

    loafers

    medium high heel shoes for women

Casual

    ethnic motif accessories for women

    knit and plaid ties for men

    loafers for men and women

    penny loafers

    low heeled shoes for women

    tennis shoes for men and women

The style of a uniform also involves what is called its "silhouette" or the lines (curved versus angular) of the constructed garment. When the uniforms you select flatter an employee's body type, he or she feels comfortable in it and projects self-confidence. As a guideline for women:

FLATTERING SILHOUETTES

1

Walking Shorts

2

3

4

5

Pleated Slacks

6

Soft Drape

7

9

10

Jewel Neck

11

8

- Select a medium-length jacket with some definition at the waist; make sure the bottom of the jacket has a slight curve.
- Avoid the angular blazer cut which makes most female bodies appear larger.
- A notched lapel with round edges or a jacket with no lapels are flattering to most body shapes.
- Select a blouse with a jewel neckline or one that is draped in a V-neck.(Be sure that the opening of the V is at least two inches above the cleavage.)
- Choose skirts that have straight lines with some give at the waist for proper fit; "A" line skirts or soft gathers are suggested for positions that require a lot of movement such as the work done by wait-staff and the housekeeping staff.
- Avoid pleated skirts which are difficult to keep pressed and neat; another drawback is that they visually add pounds to the hip area which most women try to minimize.
- The most flattering trousers for men's or women's uniforms are pleated and they also allow for comfort and ease of movement.

As a final point on style, when selecting a uniform make sure that the different elements, including the accessories, are within the same degree of dressiness or a comparable one. Use the following as a guide:

- Mix dressy with dressy and with less dressy. Example: a wool double-breasted suit, broadcloth shirt and silk tie.
- Mix less dressy with less dressy and with causal. Example: a houndstooth skirt with a vest and cotton shirt.
- Avoid mixing items that are dressy with casual since the outfit will send conflicting messages. For example: a double-breasted wool jacket with cotton buttoned-down shirt or blouse. Or, twill pants or skirt with a silk blouse or with a white shirt and silk tie.

CHOOSING THE RIGHT COLORS

Selecting the color of uniforms is one of the most challenging choices a manager has to make during the selection process. You need to consider the employee's position, the decor of the room or location where the employee will be wearing the uniform, the formality of the room and the service provided. Color is especially important when selecting uniforms for restaurants because of the emotional responses that humans have to different colors: White and pastel uniforms send a message of cleanliness. Black is considered formal, especially when used exclusively.

Color is often used in some restaurants to define internal hierarchy. There are still some fine restaurants that follow the classic French model, where a tuxedo and black bow tie usually signals captain status; a white jacket and black or white bow tie means wait-staff; and a more simply cut white jacket with or without tie means bus person. Today, many expensive restaurants choose black tuxedos or suits and white shirts for their uniforms, and they support this choice with two words—"crispness" and "tradition." The reason behind this choice is that in quality restaurants, evening is a formal time and servers should dress up to serve. However, in a casual cafe where the server is dressed in a tuxedo, the guests may feel uncomfortable. Some restaurants with quiet elegance select uniforms in soft colors such as peach, light periwinkle and aqua in order to complement their atmosphere.

We also need to consider the impact that certain colors have on the employees wearing them. For example, beige and brown will not flatter most people while turquoise and gray will flatter everyone. Let's begin by recognizing how color has an emotional, psychological and physiological effect on us. Certain colors can conjure up immediate mental images, excitement, relaxation or mood changes. Called "behaviorism" by 20th Century psychologists, the study of the response elicited by colors in the environment was launched by John Watson:

Vivid, bright color combinations suggest heat, health, vitality, humor, fun and sporting events. These colors are appropriate for health facilities, resorts and sunny places. Light and pastel colors appear soft, innocent and can lull or softly sedate the viewer.

Deep, rich colors such as purple, deep green, deep blue, brown, terra-cotta, olive green and teal have a luxurious quality. They suggest maturity, country life, mystery and haute couture.

Dark colors such as black, navy, dark brown, dark green and charcoal gray are rich, subdued, sophisticated, formal and elegant.

All colors have both their positive and their negative side. Following is one interpretation of what colors can mean:

COLOR	POSITIVE	NEGATIVE
black	*accomplished/worldly*	*empty/desolate*
blue	*secure/peaceful*	*depressing*
brown	*dependable/logical*	*plain/boring*
beige/tan	*calm/natural*	*ordinary*
burgundy	*traditional/elegant*	*over used*
blue green	*refreshing/soothing/ balancing*	*little negative effect*
cream	*calm*	*ordinary*
gray	*secure/calm*	*plain/colorless*
green	*calm/natural*	*jealous*
lilac	*approachable/gentle*	*flowery/inconsequential*
magenta/fuchsia	*memorable*	*domineering*
navy	*traditional/reliable*	*overused*
orange	*outgoing/social/fun*	*inexpensive/irritating*
peach	*friendly/safe*	*average/common*
pink	*sweet/soft*	*overly feminine*
red	*power/exciting*	*aggressive*
rust	*inviting/warm*	*too casual*
tan	*calm/natural*	*ordinary*
teal/turquoise	*refreshing/soothing*	*little negative effect*
violet	*regal*	*oppressive*
white	*pure, clean*	*lifeless*
yellow	*happy/sunny*	*stagey*

The safest colors to use are blue green, teal and turquoise. They are the only colors that rarely elicit a negative reaction from men or women. They are truly neutral says Cheryl S. Birch, author of *Color Diversity*. When Cheryl consults with hotel clients, she clarifies the message—or messages—that the company wants to project. She says that color can be used to create an identity for the entire facility or for each department. This identity is a combination of the decor colors and the colors the employees wear.

Here are three approaches:

1. The company wants to project one message throughout the facility. Perhaps they want to have an identity that is restful and safe. Their color combination could be teal and peach, with white as a neutral. The entire staff would wear a combination of teal and peach with white. Styles and fabrics would vary to go with the mood of each department. For example, front desk staff could wear teal suits, white shirts and peach and teal scarves or ties. Bell staff can wear teal with peach trim. The bistro by the pool would have wait staff wearing polo shirts and teal cotton slacks. The formal dining room staff could have a tuxedo look: black slacks, white shirt with teal cummerbund and bow tie, plus a peach flower. This would unify the entire facility and emphasize their chosen message.

2. The company wants to color code each department to create a specific mood. For example, the formal dining room staff would wear dark sophisticated colors like black, forest and burgundy. The bistro or pool area staff could wear pastel printed shirts and khakis. The front desk staff could wear traditional business colors such as gray or navy. The bell staff could wear any neutral with a red accent to make them more identifiable. This method can give the illusion to guests that they have been to many different places, though they never leave the facility. It can keep people inside instead of searching for variety outside the property.

3. Using one theme color to unify and a variety of colors to color code areas is also possible. This can be accomplished with a neutral color to which many other colors are added. For example, a facility may want to project security and, for this, gray would be a good choice. Or, they may want to project excitement and, then, red would be a good choice. Using the gray, each department would have their own color accent. Formal dining could add black and white, the front desk could add yellow or peach for friendliness and the spa could add turquoise for relaxation. When using a bright color like red, it is best to add neutrals: for the front desk it could be red with blue; in the spa, red with khaki; in the formal dining room, red with black and white, and so on.

When selecting the colors for uniforms, choose ones that emphasize recognition, helpfulness and accentuate credibility. For example, navy, a widely accepted color, will create images of honesty, trustworthiness and authoritativeness. A marine navy is best for men and royal blue or teal for women. Try gray when you are not sure what color to use; it can be used as an accent as well as the principal color. Gray works best when combined with another color.

Colors look different on each employee depending on their skin tone, but you can't go wrong when you choose one of the eleven "universal colors;" they will look good on anyone:

- marine navy (not too dark);
- off white;
- taupe (mixed with a color; avoid using it close to the face);
- warm gray (not too dark);
- teal (I call teal the women's navy of the '90s);
- turquoise;
- blue green;
- violet;
- coral;
- watermelon red;
- periwinkle.

Any version of these colors will make your employees look attractive, credible and self-assured. These choices are even more effective when selecting uniforms for employees who have more direct eye-to-eye contact with customers and guests.

Avoid colors such as brown, khaki, mustard, lime green, orange and beige for uniform items that are close to the face or for a complete garment. These colors complement only certain skin tones and will make most of your employees look tired and unattractive. Besides, most people are not even attracted to these colors, and any color that elicits a negative or lukewarm reaction will cause the wearer to feel uncomfortable or depressed. The following anecdote will illustrate this point:

When I was doing an "Image Impact" workshop for a hotel in Washington, D.C., in the late 1980s, the employees complained about their brown uniforms. "Our uniform is ugly and depressing, and we feel bad just thinking about wearing this every day," they said. New uniforms in gray and teal were on order but, as an interim solution, the manager gave the employees a "casual uniform" for the weekends when business was more relaxed and hotel guests were casually dressed. The casual uniform consisted of black slacks and a turquoise or coral (they could choose one) knit shirt. The reaction of the employees was overwhelmingly positive. The front desk employees even reported that the weekend hotel guests asked them what had happened: "You all seem happier; did you get a raise?"

Also keep in mind that colors such as light to medium gray, taupe, and tan are considered non-colors, and are so non-offensive that the person wearing them with no other color tends to disappear. Clients react to these colors in two ways, says Cheryl Birch:

1. They have a hard time identifying staff to assist them.

2. They rate the staff as poor to adequate, never superior.

Therefore, it is very important to add a colorful accent or contrast to gray, taupe, beige and tan to give employees life and identity.

If you are in charge of selecting uniforms, it's a good idea to show your employees a couple of color choices for the garments that you have selected and ask for their opinion. It is essential that you explain why you have selected the shades you are presenting to them. The blond haired, green eyed employee may prefer a yellow shirt, but once he or she understands why that color will not work for the entire team, a quicker consensus should be reached.

SELECTING THE RIGHT STYLES

The rules for business attire have been relaxing in the United States in the past few years, and the trend is toward a more friendly look rather than powerful. Uniforms are reflecting this trend of softer, more comfortable clothing. Holly Steel, the first female concierge in the United States and author of the book *Ultimate Service,* says that her first uniform as a concierge for a large hotel in San Francisco in 1974 was a suit with a shirt and tie—a replica of the male uniform. She even wore tails for formal events! Today, she

UNIFORMS THAT RESEMBLE BUSINESS ATTIRE

1

2

3

4

5

6

7

8

says, the ties and tails are gone from concierge uniforms; instead, for women, they have been replaced by coat dresses and suits in attractive colors and more feminine designs.

When we look at the trends in uniforms over the past five years, we find that uniform companies are offering options for more comfortable and wearable fabrics: washable silks, lighter wool and wool blends that look crisper and are easier to keep clean and pressed. The city uniforms are moving slightly to a more friendly hospitable look, reflecting the softness of the business look of the '90s. We are seeing more uniforms that resemble business attire and that are less regimental looking than in the past. For example, the coat dress for women instead of the blazer or suit; softer-style jackets with no lapels or shawl collars for women; suits that look feminine as well as professional. For the hostess position, many restaurants are selecting a dress uniform with a small print called *soft dressing,* since this is often what hostesses at home wear; thus, the achieved effect replicates the experience of dining in a friendly, home-like atmosphere.

By expanding the selection of shirts and ties, men's uniforms are also becoming more versatile. Striped and colored shirts are replacing the ubiquitous white when a less formal look is appropriate. Colorful ties and patterns such as medallions, dots, geometric and abstract motifs are replacing the traditional repp ties of the past. When a uniform calls for a regimental tie, bolder color combinations as well as nontraditional stripe widths are giving it a new and fresher look.

Even for the kitchen staff, uniforms reflect an up-to-date, contemporary look, with white and color combinations. Utility uniforms are now made in richer shades and stylish designs. Colorful jackets and striped shirts, blouses and aprons have replaced the neutral monochromatic color designs of the past.

Based on the new trends detailed above, it is advisable to invest in simple, well-fitting, smart-looking uniforms made of high quality material. Michael Frank, president of one of the leading uniform companies, says that selecting what he calls "cross-utilizers"—pieces that can be used for different uniforms whether pants, skirts, jackets and so forth—helps companies to save money while getting more value from their investment. "This strategy allows for investing in finer garments of higher quality fabrics and comfort," he says.

For comfort, choose a material with at least 55 percent natural fibers. Quality fabrics available for uniforms include wool crepe, cotton blends, linen cotton blends, wool gabardine and rayon. The better fabrics will wear longer and flatter more figures. Avoid styles that are "here today and gone tomorrow;" these include an extreme length for skirts, overly large prints, striped patterns or exaggerated "theme" dressing for city hotels; these styles are more appropriate for a resort look. Choose a simple, classic style that can be updated with accessories. For example, changing the tie of a man's suit uniform is an affordable way to update it. Or, adding a new blouse, scarf, necklace or pin to a woman's classic suit uniform will keep it in style. At a resort property, changing the shirt to a currently fashionable color and pattern will update any basic uniform.

Two different color blouses for women and two shirt and tie options for men will give a basic uniform flexibility and allow room for personal individuality. As an example of this flexibility, one of the major formal restaurant chains chose a well-cut classic gray suit with a bolero-style jacket embroidered with the company logo. For visual variety, different colored ties and sashes are changed seasonally. By offering accessory choices and style options to employees, you allow them to safely express their personal style while keeping your public image of excellence.

Making simple changes in uniforms will boost morale and the effectiveness of those who wear them with pride. Every two or three years uniforms can be modified slightly with accessory changes to keep them current, without having to replace them completely. To reflect the trends, though, styles and colors of uniforms should be updated every three to four years for women and every four to five years for men.

ENSURING EMPLOYEE COMFORT

Whatever color, fabric or style you select for your uniforms, it is essential that the garments are comfortable to wear. Take into consideration the temperature of the place where an employee is to work. A black uniform for an outdoor cafe in a hot and humid climate is punishment. Your employees will not only complain about the unwelcome sauna treatment but their performance will be affected as well. How can we ask someone to even smile while performing a job in such uncomfortable attire? The fiber content of the fabric needs to breathe for flexibility and comfort.

Bell staff especially need uniform flexibility as they will be exposed to both the highest and the lowest temperatures during the year. For them, two different uniforms or a uniform with interchangeable pieces to be layered according to temperature will support them in their job performance.

In addition, make sure that the style of the uniform has all the details needed to support the employees in their job. A uniform with pockets is a must for a position in which employees need to carry order books, checks, money and other essential job items. If the design of the uniform does not include pockets, a "pouch" could be added to complement the attire and be a useful and attractive accessory. Select either a neutral color that blends with the color of the pants and skirts or the same color to avoid calling attention to it.

Another important consideration when selecting uniforms is the care of the garments. Even though most properties provide dry cleaning service for employees' uniforms, it is still important to select fabrics and garments that are easy to keep clean and pressed. Also know that some colors may fade after multiple launderings and this is especially true for bright colors. When conducting a series of seminars at a resort chain in California, I thought that a group of participants in one of my seminars worked in two different departments. The style of their uniform shirts was exactly the same, but some of them were wearing bright fuchsia and others dusty rose. Then I realized that they all had the same job at the same restaurant and the older fuchsia shirt had faded to a dusty rose! To prevent this from happening, one of my clients in Virginia decided to send a printed shirt we were considering for one of

1

2

3

5

4

6

7

8

their cafes to the laundry to have it washed 100 times; then we compared it with a new one to determine how they would look side by side before making the final investment.

WORKING EFFECTIVELY WITH UNIFORM COMPANIES

The process of selecting, purchasing and caring for uniforms is complex. We interviewed the major uniform companies in the country and asked them how this process could be run smoothly and efficiently. All the companies interviewed agreed that the biggest challenge that they face when working with hospitality clients is *time.* Many times the department heads do their homework in selecting and putting a uniform program together. Unfortunately, when it comes to the decisionmakers, usually higher level executives with busy schedules, this last step slows down the process. This puts uniform companies in the position of having to deliver a uniform program in unrealistic time frames.

When there are many people involved in the selection of uniforms it makes the process more difficult. When a property has at least some ideas in mind of what they want for their uniform program, it makes the uniform company's role easier and more effective. When the process begins from ground zero, it takes additional time and energy that could be saved by bringing ideas and options to the planning meeting.

Here are some tips to help you plan and complete a cost-effective process of selecting, purchasing and caring for uniforms.

- Analyze your current uniforms: Evaluate what worked and what did not; get an idea of what you want. What is your goal? Are you looking for a complete change? Are you looking for an update? Has the property or department changed its theme? Has the decor of the property or the rooms changed? To help you with this step, read this chapter again and take some notes.
- Create the team of people that will be involved in the selection process. The smaller the team, the easier the process. More than three people may be a crowd for the initial selection.

Remember that most of the time you will need the approval of higher management, making the initial team larger.

- Decide if you will get input from the employees and, if so, how will you get them involved. Remember that it is impossible to please everyone when selecting clothes.(Just try to please all the members of your family!)

- Ask your employees what they *like and dislike* about the current uniform and really listen. You do not want to repeat the same mistakes, if there have been some in the past. Having a small team of employees representing their department to participate in this process will be useful. Show them a few alternatives and explain the reasons behind the choices. Make employees aware of issues such as: coordination with room decor, continuity of property or division theme, fabric care, flattering colors for skin tones, fashion trends and so forth. Asking a simple "Do you like it?" to a group of people without a presentation of criteria will become a struggle of differing tastes.

- It is critical that employees understand that when selecting uniforms, your options are *limited*. Most of the time there are only a few choices for a given uniform position even when you purchase from several uniform companies. Selecting uniforms is different than shopping for clothes at a department store where the choices are limitless.

- Do some pre-selection before you call the uniform company representative. It is easier for them to assist you when you have some initial ideas. Think of color and style alternatives, but be flexible! You may not find exactly what you want.

- Be realistic with time frames. After your selection process, allow time for the *decision* step, which may take longer than you plan. By now you may know how long a final decision at the executive level usually takes.

- When trying some uniform options, try them on *your own employees*. Invite two or three employees that represent sizes and body types of the group. When looking at the samples, do this analysis in the location or room where the employees will be wearing the uniforms. Bob Jeramiah, a resort manager, wears the future uniform or parts of it himself before making the final selection. When he receives compliments from his employees, he knows that is the right choice!

- Pay special attention to sizes. Sizing is a confusing world. Uniform companies would rather personally come and measure every employee than follow the measurements done in-house or from the employees' best guess. The exchanging of wrong sizes is frustrating and time consuming.

- Discuss and analyze the cleaning and maintenance issues of the planned uniforms. Prevention and planning in this area will save you time and money.

- Be open! Fashion may not be your specialty and clothing styles change. Uniform companies do extensive research of current and future fashion trends. Being close-minded may hurt the image you want for your property. Tell the vendor what you want. They can help you achieve your goals. Listen and make your own choices.

- Do not wait until the last minute when you have a significant event to select and order uniforms. The most expensive mistakes have been made in a hurry!

- Uniforms alone will not take care of the professional image of your employees. You need to complement this process with instructions on how to wear the new uniforms. Employees need to know which accessories they are supposed to wear. Give specific guidelines for shoes, socks, hose and jewelry. Look through this book for ideas. Ask professional image consultants for assistance. You will find resources in the index.

- Place full-length mirrors in locker rooms and hallways where employees circulate. This will help them to keep their uniforms and grooming updated during the day. Having grooming tools such as: toothpaste, dental floss, spray deodorant, small combs, hair spray, shoe polish and so forth available in restrooms and employee lounges will be a small investment that pays high dividends. These items will support your employees in keeping their professional image of excellence during the working hours.

It pays to do your homework before selecting uniforms. Mistakes can be very costly and long lasting, involving not only money—often thousands of dollars—but valuable time and energy as well. A poor choice also can negatively impact an employee's performance. Employees feel good when they look good and are comfortable in their uniforms; and this results in a better performance.

WEARING NAME TAGS RIGHT

In the hospitality industry, most employees wear name tags. The tag allows customers and guests to recognize and call employees by name. In addition to making the relationship more personal, it also helps the client to differentiate among the members of the various teams who are serving him or her.

Most hospitality employees wear their name tags on the left side of their chest. This custom is probably modeled after the military. In the armed forces, military personnel wear their identification and rank on the left side of their uniform jacket or shirt. This practice works well in the military because face-to-face communication takes place in a prescribed straight or "about face" body position. In this scenario, the person's identification is easy to read regardless of the side on which it is located. However, in hospitality (or any other industry except the military) we don't greet people in a squared-off straight body position, which makes it difficult when a guest or coworker is trying to read a name tag placed on the left side of the uniform. The customer must turn their head in order to read the name and, in so doing, important eye contact is broken.

When we asked numerous executives of hotels and restaurants why name tags were placed on the left, they answered that it was just a tradition that has never been questioned. Some managers told us that when the employee wears a jacket, it is easier to insert the tag in the left pocket of the jacket. Others mentioned that maybe it's easier for the employees to place their name tag on the left side of their uniform with their right hand. And others just smiled and said that the left side "is close to your heart." It seems, though, that all these reasons are employee-focused.

Name tag on left side makes it difficult for guest to read name.

Name tag on right side makes it easier for guest to read name.

In business encounters where using a person's name is essential, name tags should be placed on the right side. This allows both parties to read each others' name with ease because we read from left to right. As Michael McKinley, 1994-95 president of the National Speakers Association, says: "I always try to put my name tag on the right-hand side because it's not for me to read but each and every person I meet to comfortably read." This revised practice is now spreading rapidly throughout all industries, and it is especially important for the hospitality community to review their traditional policy in this area. By wearing our name tags on our right side, we would shift from being employee-focused to being customer-focused.

Successfully adapting this change for your organization requires planning. When Sweden decided to shift their highway system from driving on the left to driving on the right, they selected one specific day for the switch to take place around the country. The same idea works when implementing this change for your employees: Select one day and a particular time for all employees to stop for one minute and, as a symbol of courtesy to the customers, change their name tags from the left to the right side of their uniforms. Several organizations have already implemented this plan, and they report what the positive effect this shared "ceremony" has had on both their employees and their customers.

The above approach is a much better plan for implementing

this change than gradually going through the organization department by department; this might only bring confusion to employees and customers alike. This is even more important for those companies that use *gramets* on uniforms so that the name tag's pin will not rip the fabric. Ordering the graments on the right side when purchasing uniforms, will ensure that everyone in the facility will be wearing their name tag on the right side. If your company is willing to take the lead on this issue and shift from employee-focused to customer-focused communication, then planning the change for a particular day and time is worth the effort.

IN CONCLUSION

$\mathscr{B}$eing a hospitality professional is a challenge. It is more than a profession; it is a lifestyle that requires personality, charm, enthusiasm, a caring attitude and pride. It is not simple work. It is a demanding job that requires not only skills but a personal commitment. To achieve excellence in hospitality we are expected not only to serve and perform our jobs to the highest quality standards, we are expected to connect emotionally with our customers and coworkers. It means work, but it can also be fun, challenging and rewarding.

Delighting the customer means not only satisfying their needs but delivering a service that goes beyond their expectations and brings them back eager and asking for more of the same. Meeting impossible deadlines, answering questions, solving problems, fixing what is broken and finding what is lost. Soothing and calming the irate guest and reassuring the timid.

What you do is hard work. How you feel about yourself and the job you are doing—whether you love it or are overwhelmed by it—will reflect in your performance. You probably know how all these demands can cause daily stress. Therefore, you must take care of yourself. You cannot take care of your customers if you do not take care of yourself first. Know your limits. Only you can manage the way you react to the multiple demands that your hospitality job requires. When you feel stressed out, do something about it. Do not let stress accumulate to the point that it affects your performance and your relationships at work and at home. Learn to breathe deeply; it is one of the most unused stress reducers. Laugh and maintain a sense of humor. As a friend of mine says, "Every drama has its ridiculous part." Learn to laugh at yourself; it's good medicine. Stretch, move, take a walk, take two days off in a row, take time to unwind, take a one-minute mental vacation to your favorite place during your work day—do something that gives you pleasure. In other words, celebrate a job well done.

After reading this book you probably found that many of the things that you are doing are reinforcing your professional image and performance. You may also like to make some changes. Some of these changes will be easy and quick to implement; others may need a commitment in order to become a habit. This may take some attention and time, but it will be well worth it. Remember, that it takes:

> 5 seconds to make an impression
> 21 days to start a pattern
> 100 days for a pattern to become a habit.

Realize that what you do is very important. Regardless of what your position is in the organization—whether you serve the guest directly or serve those who serve the guest—you are in the business of customer satisfaction. The entire organization's success depends on *you* doing your job well, thoughtfully, skillfully and to the customer's delight. It all comes down to *you!* The way you look is important. What you say is important. What you do is important. How you feel is important. All of these comprise your Professional Image of Excellence.

The success of your career and your company begins and ends with YOU!

APPENDIX

Answers to the Men's Clothing IQ.

1. Yes. When combining two stripes—tie and suit—the width of the stripes should be different. Black lace-up shoes are appropriate for this dressy outfit.

2. No. The combination of suit, shirt, tie and braces is correct. No matching pocket square. A solid blue or red pocket square will make the outfit work.

3. No. A black suit is not appropriate for daytime. If you need to look powerful, select a dark navy or gray suit. Black is only for evening wear.

4. No. A pin-dot tie is too dressy for a tweed suit. Changing it for a wool or a paisley tie will make the outfit work better. Besides, no clip on the tie; clips ruin your ties and are outdated.

5. No. No short sleeves with suits, and no shoes with buckles for work.

6. Yes. This is an appropriate look for a resort property. The fabrics and colors are compatible.

7. Yes. This is a dressy look for an evening event. Notice that all the pieces are in the dressy category: dark suit, tone-on-tone French-cuffed shirt, woven micro-patterned tie. The black-and-white pocket square adds pizzazz to the look.

8. Yes. The combination is correct, and it is advisable to wear a tie with some tone of red when you make presentations, since it attracts attention to your face.

ANSWERS TO THE WOMEN'S CLOTHING IQ.

1. No. Pure linen is a fabric that wrinkles too much, damaging your professional appearance. Suntan hose are not appropriate; they make your legs look orange. When wearing black shoes during the summer months, select hose in your skin tone for a more blended, softer look.

2. No. When wearing a dark hemline like navy, you look more professional with darker shoes; navy or black would be a better selection. Then, hose in gray or your skin tone will complement the look. Please note that a navy suit is a good choice when you want to look powerful. The wrong combination of shoes and hose will bring too much attention to your legs.

3. Yes. The key piece of the outfit is the jacket. The jacket makes the dress dressy enough for an important meeting. The small print of the dress is also very appropriate for business. Shoes and hose complement the outfit.

4. No. The outfit is too dressy for business. A silk floral dress sends conflicting messages at the office since it is appropriate for social occasions only. An open neckline is not recommended either for a polished professional look.

5. No. For a presentation you want to wear a jacket. Besides, the dangling earrings are not appropriate for business. With different earrings, this outfit will be a smart choice for a regular day at work.

6. Yes. This is a very appropriate and smart business look.

7. No. When you meet a client for the first time, you want to wear a jacket. Keeping a jacket at the office will take care of instantly upgrading an outfit like this to a more professional look.

PERCEPTIONS CREATED BY WOMEN'S OUTFITS

1. **a** Client relates to a competent business look. Reinforces confidence in doing business with company.

2. **b** Client senses a "sporty" loose feeling about the company. Lack of seriousness to handle his/her business.

3. **d** An outdated look may reflect lack of innovation in the marketplace.

4. **a** Client relates to a competent business look. Reinforces confidence in doing business with company.

5. **c** Client may interpret this as a social occasion, not a business opportunity.

ANSWERS TO THE BUSINESS ETIQUETTE IQ.

1. **No.** The most important person's name—in this case, Mr. Anderson, your client—should be the one you say first. The correct introduction is: "Mr. Anderson (your client), I want to introduce Ms. Brown, our director of marketing."

2. **Yes.** Men do not have to wait for women to initiate a handshake in business today. Both men and women can initiate a handshake in a work situation.

3. **b** Regardless of gender, it is courteous to rise when a visitor enters a room.

4. **No.** In an elevator, the person closest to the door, regardless of gender, will exit first. If the elevator is crowded, the person closest to the door will step out to let others leave, even if that is not the floor of his or her destination.

5. **c** Leave your napkin on the chair. This is a message to the wait staff that you will come back. Leaving your napkin loosely folded on the right side of the table means you are finished with your meal and you are leaving the table for good.

6. **c** Today it is recommended not to drink any alcoholic beverages during luncheon meetings. If your client is from another country in which drinking is appropriate, you may want to have one glass of wine served to make your client feel comfortable. However, you do not have to drink it all.

7. **c** Cut one small piece at a time and butter it on the plate before eating it.

8. **No.** It is inappropriate to conduct any grooming activities at the dining table regardless of gender. How would you react if a

man in a business setting took out his small electric shaver and shaved at the table after a meal?

9. Fax machines should be used only for exchange of information. Personal business notes for thank yous, congratulations, condolences, and so forth, should be mailed to keep them personal.

10. a Meetings conducted at round tables are more effective. People reach agreement easier and faster than at any other type of table configuration.

RESOURCES

Tie Trap (a ribbon with buttonholes to keep your tie in place) is distributed by Capriccio in Illinois. For orders call: 708-443-9476

JoS.A.Bank—For orders call: 1-800-2855-2265

Barrie Pace Ltd.—For orders call: 1-800-441-6011

Angelica Uniforms—For orders call: 1-800-222-3112

Uniforms To You—For orders call: 1-800-864-3676

SEMINARS, PRESENTATIONS AND INDIVIDUAL COACHING

For more information about the author's and her consultants' seminars, presentations and personal coaching, please contact:

Image Resource Group, Inc.
7809 Wincanton Court
Falls Church, VA 22043
Phone: 703-560-3950
Fax: 703-573-8904

BIBLIOGRAPHY

PROFESSIONAL DRESS— MEN AND WOMEN

Dressing to Win, Robert Pante (Doubleday)

The Power of Dress, Jacqueline Murray (Semiotics)

The Professional Image, Susan Bixler (Putnam)

PROFESSIONAL DRESS—MEN

Clothes and the Man, Alan Flusser (Villard Books)

Dress for Excellence, Lois Fenton (Rawson Associates)

Elegance, G. Bruce Boyer (Norton)

Presenting Yourself, Mary Spillane (Piatkus)

Red Socks Don't Work, Kenneth J. Karpinski (Impact)

Successful Style, Doris Pooser (HDL Publishing)

The Executive Look, Mortimer Levitt (Atheneum)

You Are What You Wear, William Thourlby (Forbes/Wittenburg & Brown)

PROFESSIONAL DRESS—WOMEN

Color to Color: The Black Woman's Guide to a Rainbow of Fashion and Beauty, Jean E. Patton (Fireside/Simon & Schuster)

Color with Style, Donna Fujii (Graphic-Sha Publishing
Company, Ltd.)

Looking Terrific, Emily Cho (Ballantine Books)

Looking, Working, Living Terrific, Emily Cho
(Ballantine Books)

Presenting Yourself: A Personal Image Guide for Women,
Mary Spillane (Piatkus)

Secrets of Style, Doris Pooser (Crisp Publications, Inc.)

The Complete Style Guide, Mary Spillane (Piatkus)

The Extra Edge: A Woman's Guide to Total Professional Style,
Charlene Mitchell (Acropolis Books)

The Triumph of Individual Style, Carla Mason Mathis and
Helen Villa Connor (Timeless Editions)

Working Wardrobe, Janet Wallach (Acropolis Books)

CUSTOMER SERVICE

Beyond the Bottom Line, Tad Tuleja (Penguin Books)

Delivering Knock Your Socks Off Service, Kristin Anderson
and Ron Zemke (American Management Association)

How to Read People Like a Book (Audio Tape), Maxine
McIntyre (7286 E. El Caminito Dr., Scottsdale, AZ 85258)

How to Win Customers and Keep Them for Life,
Michael LeBoeuf (Berkley Books)

Service America, Karl Albrecht and Ron Zemke
(Dow Jones-Irwin)

Service Wisdom, Ron Zemke and Chip R. Bell
(Lakewood Books)

The Real Heroes of Business and Not a CEO Among Them,
Bill Fromm and Len Schlesinger (Currency-Doubleday)

Ultimate Service, Holly Stiel and Delta Collins
(Regents/Prentice Hall)

BODY LANGUAGE

Lions Don't Need to Roar, D. A. Benton (Warner Books)

Professional Presence, Susan Bixler (Putnam)

Silent Messages, Albert Mehrabian (Wadsworth)

Subtext, Julius Fast (Viking)

BUSINESS ETIQUETTE

Business Protocol, Jan Yager (John Wiley & Sons, Inc.)

Corporate Protocol, Valerie Grant-Sokolosky (Honor/
   Harrison House)

Diccionario de la Etiqueta, Evelia Porto (Ediciones
   Gamma S.A.)

Dos and Taboos of Hosting International Visitors,
   Roger E. Axtell (John Wiley & Sons, Inc.)

El Arte de la Etiqueta, Evelia Porto de Mejia
   (Ediciones Gamma)

It's Fun to Entertain, Blackie Scott (Peachtree Publishers, Ltd.)

Letitia Baldrige's Complete Guide to Executive Manners
   (Rawson Associates)

Miss Manners' Guide for the Turn-of-the-Millennium, Judith
   Martin (Pharos Books/Scripps Howard Co.)

The Amy Vanderbilt Complete Book of Etiquette (Doubleday)

The Traveler's Guide to European Customs & Manners,
   Nancy L. Braganti and Elizabeth Devine (Meadowbrook)

The World-Class Executive, Neil Chesanow (Rawson Associates)

BUSINESS MANAGEMENT

The Fifth Discipline, Peter M. Senge (Currency/Doubleday)

Winning the Image Game, Bobbie Gee (PageMill Press)

SELF MANAGEMENT

The Seven Habits of Highly Effective People, Stephen R. Covey
   (Fireside/Simon & Schuster)

PHOTOS AND ILLUSTRATIONS CREDITS